THOMAS
JEFFERSON
AND THE
TRIPOLI PIRATES

THOMAS JEFFERSON
AND THE
TRIPOLI PIRATES

The War That Changed American History

Brian Kilmeade & Don Yaeger

VIKING

Viking

An imprint of Penguin Random House LLC, New York

First published in the United States of America by Viking,
an imprint of Penguin Random House LLC, 2020.

Visit us online at penguinrandomhouse.com

LIBRARY OF CONGRESS CATALOGING-IN-PUBLICATION DATA IS AVAILABLE
ISBN 9780425288955

Printed in the United States of America

10 9 8 7 6 5 4 3 2 1

To all the history teachers, American reenactors, museum curators
in every corner of this country determined to keep
America's remarkable history alive.
—BK

To my favorite young readers—Will and Maddie!
Your time spent in books is never wasted
and always inspiring. I love you both!
—DY

Peace and friendship with all mankind is our wisest policy, and I wish we may be permitted to pursue it. But the temper and folly of our enemies may not leave this in our choice.

—Thomas Jefferson to C. W. F. Dumas, 1786

Contents

Note to Our Readers

Dear reader,

Every Fourth of July we celebrate our country's independence, often with barbeques, parades, fireworks, and quality time with family and friends. On July 4th, it's hard not to picture our founding fathers signing the Declaration of Independence in Philadelphia, or the brave heroes who sacrificed their lives in the name of the revolution. But have you ever stopped to think about what occurred in the years that followed the end of the war? It wasn't always smooth sailing for the new country—in fact, quite the opposite.

Imagine being told to work on a group project without receiving any instructions or help from your teacher. It would be chaos! First, you'd have to work out a strategy with your classmates, who probably wouldn't always agree with each other. You might have a few arguments, and you'd certainly make plenty of mistakes along the way. But in the end, your grade would depend on everyone working together to develop a finished product you could all be proud of.

That's just what it was like for the people governing America in its early stages of independence—Thomas Jefferson among them. As president, he didn't always have all the answers, and not everyone agreed with his tactics. But he showed impressive leadership when the country needed it most, doing his best to make smart decisions for the future of the nation. He didn't just want America to work, he wanted it to be the best it could possibly be. Just as you'd want your project to be the best in order to earn that A+.

Establishing a country from scratch is no easy task. It took a whole lot of trial and error, and ups and downs to achieve success. And with no guidance or support from its former "parent," Great Britain, for the first time ever, the U.S. had to deal with some very complicated challenges on its own.

Thinking of today's America, it might be difficult to imagine the country ever struggling to be recognized as a dominant presence. But like you and me, it had to learn and gain experience. The nation went through a tough period of transition, with growing pains and bumps and bruises along the way. But in the end, its people worked together toward making America one of the most powerful countries in the world, a legacy that has lasted through the present day.

I hope when you read this book, you'll have a newfound appreciation for the people who took part in not only winning America's independence, but building its international status. The United States has always been at the forefront of innovation, and it's all because some of the brightest minds of the time came together to win our freedom, and made America a place where we can thrive as a people.

Happy reading!
Brian

Cast of Characters

John Adams: Minister to the Court of St. James's, later President of the United States

William Bainbridge: Captain, U.S. Navy

Joel Barlow: Consul General to the Barbary States

Samuel Barron: Captain, U.S. Navy, commander of the USS *President*

Salvador Catalano: Pilot, USS *Intrepid*

James Leander Cathcart: U.S. Consul to Tripoli

Richard Dale: Captain, U.S. Navy

Stephen Decatur Jr.: Lieutenant, U.S. Navy

William Eaton: U.S. Consul General to Tunis

Hassan: Dey of Algiers until 1798

Martha and Mary (Polly) Jefferson: Daughters of Thomas Jefferson

Thomas Jefferson: Minister to France, later President of the United States

Tobias Lear: U.S. Consul General to the Barbary States

James Madison: Secretary of State, later President of the United States

Richard Valentine Morris: Captain, U.S. Navy, commander of the USS *Chesapeake*

Alexander Murry: Captain, U.S. Navy, commander of the USS *Constellation*

Bobba Mustapha: Dey of Algiers as of January 1799

Nicholas Nissen: Danish Consul General

Presley Neville O'Bannon: Lieutenant, U.S. Marines

Richard O'Brien: Captain of the *Dauphin*

Edward Preble: Captain, U.S. Navy, commander of the USS *Constitution*

Hamet Qaramanli: Brother of Yusuf and rightful heir as Bashaw of Tripoli

Yusuf Qaramanli: Bashaw of Tripoli

Mahomet Rous: Admiral, Navy of Tripoli, commander of the *Tripoli*

Andrew Sterett: Lieutenant, U.S. Navy, commander of the USS *Enterprise*

Maulay Sulaiman: Sultan of Morocco

George Washington: President of the United States

Prologue: *It Was a Sight He Would Never Forget*

As a fast-moving ship approached the *Dauphin* off the coast of Portugal, Captain Richard O'Brien saw no cause for alarm. On this warm July day in 1785, America was at peace, and there were many innocent reasons for a friendly ship to come alongside. Perhaps it was a fellow merchant ship needing information or supplies. Perhaps the ship's captain wanted to warn him of nearby pirates.

By the time O'Brien realized that the ship did not approach in peace, it was too late. The American ship was no match for the Algerian vessel armed with fourteen cannons. A raiding party with daggers gripped between their teeth swarmed over the sides of the *Dauphin*. The Algerians vastly outnumbered the American crew and quickly claimed the ship and all its goods in the name of the dey, the Algerian ruler.

Mercilessly, the pirates stripped O'Brien and his men of shoes, hats, and handkerchiefs, leaving them unprotected from the burning sun during the twelve-day voyage back to the North African coast. On arrival in Algiers, the American captives were paraded through the streets as spectators jeered.

The seamen were issued rough sets of Algerian clothing and two blankets each that were meant to last the entire period of captivity, whether it was a few weeks or fifty years. Kept in a fenced-in slave

Desert uniform worn by French troops in North Africa, 1846.

pen, they slept on a stone floor, gazing into the night sky. Each night there was a roll call, and any man who failed to respond promptly would be chained to a column and whipped soundly in the morning.

Together with men of another captured ship, the *Maria*, O'Brien's *Dauphin* crew spent their days breaking boulders into rubble in the mountains, their hands shackled with iron chains. They worked this way Saturday through Thursday. On Friday, the Muslim holy day, the prisoners dragged massive sleds loaded with rubble nearly two miles to the harbor to be unloaded into the sea to form a breakwater, a submerged wall to protect the harbor from ocean waves. Their workdays began before the sun rose, and for a few blissfully cool hours, they worked in darkness.

Their diet consisted of stale bread, vinegar from a shared bowl at breakfast and lunch, and, on good days, some ground olives. Water was the one necessity provided in abundance. As a ship captain, O'Brien was treated somewhat better, but he feared that his men would starve to death. O'Brien was allowed to write letters and receive visitors.

"Our sufferings are beyond our expression or your conception," O'Brien wrote to America's minister to France, Thomas Jefferson, two weeks after his arrival in Algiers. Those sufferings would only get worse. Several of the captives from the *Maria* and the *Dauphin* would die in captivity of yellow fever, overwork, or exposure—and in some ways, they were the lucky ones. The ways out of prison for the remaining prisoners were few: convert to Islam, attempt to escape, or wait for their country to negotiate their release. A few of the captives would be ransomed, but for most, freedom remained out of reach as their thin blankets wore out year after year. Richard O'Brien would be ten years a slave.

America had not yet elected its first president, but it already had its first enemy.

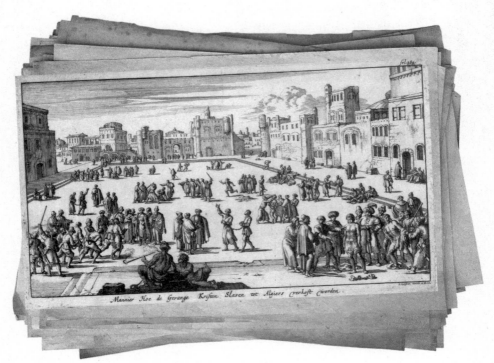

Prisoners for sale in a marketplace in Algiers in 1684.

Part
One

CHAPTER 1

1783: Wealth Travels by Sea

The United States, having won independence from Great Britain in the Revolutionary War, was a small nation positioned from the coast of the Atlantic Ocean on the east, to the Great Lakes to the north, and to the Mississippi River on the west. The land claimed by the new nation was the property of the native peoples who had lived on it for generations. Some of this land had been bought, some had been fought over, most had been taken unceremoniously. In addition, Spain claimed territory to the south and west of the country, as did Great Britain to the north.

Before the Revolution, merchant ships carrying goods to sell in Europe had been protected by British warships and, during the war, by French ships. But those arrangements were over. Now, American ships had to fend for themselves—and the new country did not yet have a navy.

The Revolution had been fought with money borrowed from

France and the Netherlands, and repayment of those debts depended upon ongoing international commerce. One key piece of the nation's economic health was trade with southern Europe, accessible only by sailing across the Atlantic Ocean, through the Strait of Gibraltar, and into the Mediterranean Sea. One-quarter of New England's most important export, dried salt cod, went to markets there, as did one-sixth of the country's grain. Rice and lumber were also important, and the merchant ships provided employment for more than a thousand seamen. Trade and employment were essential to the growing American economy, and that meant sending ships into international waters.

The busy harbor of Boston, Massachusetts, with the city in the background, in 1723.

Merchant ships did not carry cannons or ammunition. It was understood that if a ship did not have weapons, it could not be considered an enemy ship. In a conflict or war, one side might stop a merchant ship, refuse it passage, or even sink it after removing the crew, but the merchant ship would not be fired upon without warning. However, this code did not apply to pirates, and so these merchant ships, sailing from the new United States without any military vessels to escort them through international waters, were especially vulnerable.

CHAPTER 2

Centuries-Old Practice

The nations along the northern coast of Africa that border the Mediterranean Sea were known until the nineteenth century as the Barbary States. The name "Barbary" refers to the Berber people, who were the original inhabitants of much of North Africa. The region then contained the countries of Morocco, Algiers, Tunis, and Tripoli.

Pirates from the region had preyed on foreign shipping for centuries, attacking ships in international waters in the Mediterranean Sea, along the northwest coast of Africa, and along the Iberian Peninsula, off the coasts of Portugal and Spain.

Since at least the sixteenth century, the pirates had been turning over their booty to the nations' leaders to enhance their wealth. A portion of the profits were sent to Constantinople (today Istanbul) as tribute to the Ottoman rulers, the recognized overlords of the Mohammedan world; a smaller portion went to the parties who made the capture; and the remainder became the property of the local ruler. The pirates made their money from selling stolen goods and captured sailors as slaves.

Even such naval powers as France and Great Britain were not immune to the threat of piracy, though they chose to deal with the problem by paying annual "gifts" to Barbary leaders—bribes paid to the Barbary States to persuade the pirates to leave their merchant ships alone. But the prices were always changing, and the ships of those nations that did not meet the exorbitant demands were not safe from greedy pirates.

Clothing worn by Moroccan men and women in the 1800s.

By 1783, the growing wealth of the United States had caught the pirates' attention. No longer would they attack just the American vessels unlucky enough to cross their path; they were now actively seeking out American ships.

CHAPTER 3

For Jefferson, the Issue Is Personal

Thomas Jefferson had sailed for Europe in the summer of 1784 with his daughter Martha, whom he called "Patsy," to act as a trade commissioner. He joined John Adams and Benjamin Franklin, the United States' minister to France at the time. Together, they were to negotiate trade agreements with European countries. In Paris, Jefferson enrolled his daughter in a convent school with many other wellborn, English-speaking students. There he would be able to visit her regularly, though he had been forced to make a more difficult decision regarding Martha's two younger sisters. Mary, not yet six, and toddler Lucy Elizabeth, both too young to travel with their father across the sea, had been left behind with their "Aunt Eppes," his late wife's half sister. The separation was painful, but it was nothing compared with the heartbreak he experienced just months into his Paris stay when Mrs. Eppes wrote sadly to say that "hooping cough" had taken the life of two-year-old Lucy.

As a fresh wave of sorrow rolled over him, Jefferson longed for "Polly the Parrot," as he affectionately called his bright and talkative Mary, to join his household again. The father wrote to his little girl that he and her sister "cannot live without you" and asked her if she would like to join them across the ocean. He promised that coming to France meant she would learn "to play on the harpsichord, to draw, to dance, to read and talk French."

Thomas Jefferson

Jefferson began to plan for her safe travel. Having already lost his wife and one child, he did not want to risk losing Polly, and looked for ways to reduce the dangers of the journey. He instructed her uncle, Francis Eppes, to select a proven ship for Polly's crossing. "The vessel should have performed one [transatlantic] voyage at least," Jefferson ordered, "and must not be more than four or five years old." He worried about the weather and insisted that his daughter travel in the warmer months to avoid winter storms. As for supervision, Polly could make the journey, Jefferson advised, "with some good lady passing from America to France, or even England . . . [or] a careful gentleman."

Yet an even more intimidating concern worried Jefferson:

more frightening than weather or leaky ships was the threat of pirates.

Polly would not sail to Paris for several more years, and when she did, her trip was uneventful. But the awful worry Jefferson felt as he imagined an encounter between his daughter and pirates stayed with him even after her safe arrival.

CHAPTER 4

The Two Ambassadors

In 1785, Benjamin Franklin returned to the United States to become the president of the executive council of the state of Pennsylvania, a job similar to that of a governor today. Thomas Jefferson took his place as minister to France, and that same year, John Adams was named the country's first ambassador to Great Britain.

In early 1786, the two friends Jefferson and Adams met in London to discuss several matters, including how to deal with an emerging threat to American interests: piracy.

Fifty-year-old John Adams welcomed Jefferson into his London home. Overlooking the tree-lined Grosvenor Square from the town house Adams had rented, the two men sat down to talk in the spacious drawing room.

Unlike most of the European diplomats they encountered, neither Adams nor Jefferson had been born into a tradition of diplomatic decorum. Adams was a rough-and-tumble lawyer, the son of a farmer

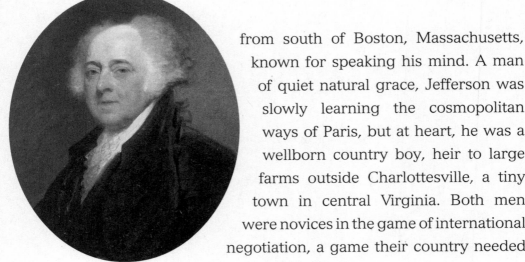

John Adams

from south of Boston, Massachusetts, known for speaking his mind. A man of quiet natural grace, Jefferson was slowly learning the cosmopolitan ways of Paris, but at heart, he was a wellborn country boy, heir to large farms outside Charlottesville, a tiny town in central Virginia. Both men were novices in the game of international negotiation, a game their country needed them to learn quickly.

When the Americans and British signed the Treaty of Paris back in 1783, bringing an end to the Revolution, the United States' legal status changed in the view of every nation and world leader. No longer under British protection, the fledgling nation found that its status was lowly indeed. Even two years after their arrival in London, Adams's letters to the British government tended to go unanswered, and Jefferson's attempts to negotiate trade treaties with France and Spain were going nowhere. Now a more hostile international threat was rearing its head, and Adams had summoned Jefferson from Paris to discuss the danger posed by the pirates of North Africa.

In the United States, trade was booming. But John Adams thought trade numbers could easily improve even more if a diplomatic solution in the Barbary region could be reached.

Adams and Jefferson worried over the fate of the *Dauphin* and the *Maria*. It had been nearly a year since the pirates from Algiers had taken the ships and cargoes, and now the regent of Algiers had made known his demand: until he was paid an exorbitant and, it seemed, ever-escalating ransom, the American captives were to remain his slaves.

The American government had initially approved payment to the North African nations. But the bribes demanded were impossibly high, many hundreds of thousands of dollars, when the American treasury could afford only token offerings of a few tens of thousands. In an era when not a single American was worth one million dollars, paying such excessive bribes seemed almost incomprehensible. Unable to pay enough to buy the goodwill of the Barbary countries, America was forced to let its ships sail at their own risk. Sailors like those on the *Maria* and the *Dauphin* had become pawns in a very dangerous game.

Despite their pity for the captives, Jefferson and Adams knew the young nation couldn't afford another war or a new source of debt. They also understood that the cost of keeping American ships away from the Barbary Coast would be greater than the cost of addressing the problem. That left the two American ministers, as Jefferson confided to a friend, feeling "absolutely suspended between indignation and impotence."

Yet neither Jefferson nor Adams could afford to remain paralyzed in the face of the danger. Not only had American families and the economy been endangered, but rumor had it that the pirates had also captured a ship carrying the venerable Benjamin Franklin, Jefferson's predecessor as minister to France. (As one correspondent wrote to Franklin, "We are waiting with the greatest patience to hear

Benjamin Franklin, in a portrait published in 1778.

from you. The newspapers have given us anxiety on your account; for some of them insist that you have been taken by the Algerines, while others pretend that you are at Morocco, enduring your slavery with all the patience of a philosopher.") To everyone's relief, the reports proved false, but the scare brought the very real dangers posed by the Barbary pirates too close for comfort.

Sitting in Adams's London house, John Adams and Thomas Jefferson discussed the idea of a negotiation that might break the impasse. The two ministers set about deciding upon the right approach.

CHAPTER 5

Jefferson and Adams Disagree

In the coming months, the two old friends would find they disagreed about how to deal with the Barbary pirates. Adams remained determined to continue the negotiations. The Americans should be willing to pay for peace, he believed, even if they had to borrow money to pay the tributes. "If it is not done," he wrote to Jefferson from London, "you and I . . . ought to go home."

Back in Paris, Jefferson expressed another view. He did not wish to "buy a peace," as he put it. He did not trust the Barbary powers to keep their word. At the same time, he did not think America could afford to stop trading with the European countries on the Mediterranean. He believed in freedom on the seas, and he proposed a tougher position.

"I should prefer the obtaining of it by war," he wrote to Adams from France in 1786. Jefferson argued that America needed a navy to confront and destroy the pirates of the Barbary Coast. The fifty ships that had defended the colonies during the Revolutionary War had been sold off at the end of the war to raise money for the new country.

Jefferson told Adams that justice, honor, and the respect of Europe for the United States would be served by establishing a fleet in "constant cruise" in Barbary waters, policing and confronting ships of the outlaw states as necessary. He argued that an armed naval presence made budgetary sense. According to his calculations, establishing a small navy would be less costly than the sum of the ransoms, bribes, and maritime losses.

Adams disagreed. He believed that a war against the Barbary nations could be unwinnable, and that it would certainly require too large a military force for America's budget. Opposing Jefferson's belief that a small navy could solve the problem, he told Jefferson, "We ought not to fight them at all unless We determine to fight them forever."

CHAPTER

Leaders for a New Nation

Adams and his family returned to Massachusetts in April 1788. One year later, on April 30, 1789, George Washington was elected the first president of the United States. Adams won the election for vice president. It had been five years since winning the war against England and signing a peace treaty. National leaders had been meeting in Philadelphia to discuss, argue over, and revise a constitution for the new country. The document was ratified in 1788, clearing the way for the election of the first president.

Thomas Jefferson and his daughters returned from France in 1789. Jefferson discovered that while on shipboard, he had been chosen to be secretary of state in the administration.

Jefferson was both humbled and honored that George Washington had appointed him for the daunting task. Except for matters of finance and war, the secretary of state would administer the entire government. Jefferson asked for time to consider the offer, but back

Thomas Jefferson's daughter Martha Jefferson Randolph.

at home that winter in central Virginia, he decided to accept the appointment. He remained at his mountaintop home, Monticello, to witness the February marriage of daughter Martha, now seventeen, before traveling to New York, temporarily the nation's capital, to join the government.

At their very first meeting, on March 22, 1790, the president and his new secretary of state discussed an issue that had been weighing on Jefferson for years: the plight of Richard O'Brien and his men.

Washington and Jefferson weren't the only Americans worrying about their captive countrymen. On May 14, 1790, a letter from the captured men was read on the Congress floor, asking the representatives to intervene on their behalf as their situation grew more desperate and the outlook even bleaker as the years passed.

Congress's interest in the problem went beyond the enslaved men. Due to the continuing threat to ships, American trade in the Mediterranean was dwindling—at a great cost to the otherwise thriving American economy. Congress and the president wasted no time, immediately referring the matter to the new secretary of state. With Washington's mandate, Jefferson set about examining the issue in detail.

A bookish man by nature, Jefferson began by looking into the history of the Barbary pirates. He planned to spend months researching the pirates' centuries-long practice of enslaving innocent sailors before making definitive suggestions for action. As he compiled an exhaustive report on the problem, he also corresponded with Richard O'Brien, who remained a prisoner of the Algerians.

Because O'Brien had the rank of sea captain, his experience in captivity was far better than that of most other prisoners, and he had been assigned relatively comfortable work at the British consulate, tilling soil, planting trees, and feeding the pigs before eventually rising to become a liaison to the dey of Algiers. That privileged position allowed him to travel to Portugal, England, and Germany to beg for ransom gold from governments, private parties, and Christian aid groups. He was heavily guarded on such journeys, so he was unable to make his escape. He also knew that if he did not return, things would become much worse for the men he left behind—men who were already subjected to hard labor and harsh treatment.

O'Brien did what he could to answer the questions Jefferson posed to him in his letters, and on December 30, 1790, President Washington laid before both houses of Congress the results of Jefferson's meticulous research. There were two reports, titled "Prisoners at Algiers" and "Mediterranean Trade."

Although his research seemed to support the strategy of paying ransom, Jefferson had his doubts. He maintained his long-standing skepticism about the idea of purchasing peace. For years, even before the capture of the *Dauphin* and the *Maria* and his subsequent disagreement with Adams, Jefferson had called for America to establish a navy to solve the problem of the Barbary pirates. Seven years prior, he had written of his objections to paying tribute. If negotiations broke down—as indeed they had, repeatedly, in the past—what then? "If they refuse a [fair treaty], why not go to war with them? We ought to begin a naval power if we mean to carry on our own commerce. Can we begin it on a more honorable occasion, or with a weaker foe? I am of opinion [that] with half a dozen frigates [we could] totally destroy their commerce."

In his 1790 reports to Congress, the ever-thorough Jefferson presented detailed intelligence on the size of the naval force at Algiers and its tactics. He wasn't impressed with the Algerians' poorly equipped ships, pointing out that their battle strategy depended on boarding their target ships rather than on their cannons. He hinted that the Americans would need only a small navy to beat the pirates who had commandeered the *Dauphin*, but perhaps caving to political pressure, he stopped short of calling for direct military action. "It rests with Congress to decide between war, tribute, and ransom," he concluded, "as the means of re-establishing our Mediterranean commerce."

Some senators considered instituting a navy, but the nation's empty treasury ended the conversation about warships before it got started. Ransom seemed cheaper, but the process for funding it was excruciatingly slow; it wasn't until more than a year later, in 1792, that the sum of $40,000 was authorized for ransom as part of a treaty with Algiers. Then distance and death increased the delay—the two men appointed to negotiate with Algiers both died of natural causes before talks could begin—so it wasn't until 1794 that any negotiations started.

Meanwhile, O'Brien and his men, enslaved for nine years, still waited for freedom.

CHAPTER 7

Jefferson Builds a Navy

When Jefferson became secretary of state in 1790, his nation had no navy to speak of. The last of the ships in the Continental Navy—the ships that had fought the British in the Revolutionary War—had been sold off after the Revolution. There had been no money to maintain them, and no threat close enough to home to justify raising funds.

The dismantling of the navy had suited President Washington perfectly. He made it clear that he favored a policy of strict neutrality in international affairs. Recalling the terrible toll of the Revolution on the nation's people and resources, Washington wished to fight no more wars. He desired neither a standing army nor a navy.

That Washington and Jefferson did not see eye to eye on many issues was one of the worst-kept secrets in Philadelphia. Based on his earlier years in Europe, Jefferson believed sound judgment on the Barbary situation called for military action. He would submit to his president but push where he could.

His influence seems to have worked. A matter of months after Jefferson joined the cabinet, the political tide began to turn. In October 1793, the secretary of state received a desperate letter from the U.S. consul in Lisbon, Portugal. A new attack fleet, or flotilla, of Algerian ships roamed the Atlantic near Gibraltar, a peninsula on the southern coast of Spain that was part of the British Empire. The flotilla consisted of eight ships, including four frigates and a twenty-gun brig. Their objective? "To cruise against the American flag." "I have not slept since Receipt of the news of this hellish plot," the consul wrote Jefferson. "Another corsair [pirate] in the Atlantic—God preserve us—."

Soon a new dispatch from Gibraltar reported that ten American vessels had been captured in late October. Not only had the Algerians taken more ships, but they had also added 110 captives to their slave pens. The pirate problem could be ignored no longer, nor simply be debated. Action was required.

In Congress, a House committee was appointed to study the sort of ships that would be effective in battle against the pirates. The committee soon reported back, and the House debate began on February 16, 1794, and lasted a full month. Jefferson's own Republican party—led by his dear friend and confidant James Madison, at that time a congressman—took a stance different from Jefferson's, believing that a navy would unnecessarily expand the federal government. The other party, the Federalists, used Jefferson's old argument, and reasoned that the cost of establishing a navy would be less than the cost of not having one. Maritime insurance rates continued to skyrocket, and the cost of imported goods grew by the

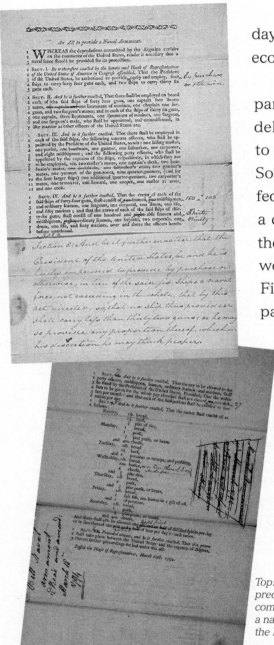

day. A navy, they argued, had become economically necessary.

Despite the bitter division between parties and regions—New England delegates tended to want a navy to protect their merchants while Southerners generally opposed such federal expansion—the House reached a compromise. The work of building the ships could begin, but construction would stop if peace were negotiated. Finally, both houses of Congress passed the Act to Provide a Naval Armament by narrow margins. Signed into law by President Washington on March 27, 1794, the act authorized the purchase or construction of six frigates, four rated for forty-four guns, two for thirty-six guns. The immense sum of $688,888 was appropriated.

Top: The Naval Act of 1794, page 1: "Whereas the predations committed by the Algerian corsairs on the commerce of the United States, render it necessary that a naval force be provided for its protection." Passed by the House of Representatives on March 10, 1794.

Bottom: Page 2 of the Naval Act of 1794 lists the food and drink that will be provided to the sailors on each day of the week.

Thus it had been decided: the United States would have a navy. George Washington ordered the shipbuilding contracts to be spread out between northern and southern ports, and construction began. Three years would pass before the first frigate was launched, and during that time, the chess match that was Barbary diplomacy would see the rules of the game shift again and again. With every failed negotiation, it became increasingly clear that only one solution remained: the new frigates would have to cross the ocean and try a different kind of diplomacy, one that came from the mouths of their cannons.

An unfinished portrait of George Washington by Gilbert Stuart. Stuart painted this from life and used it as the basis for more than seventy-five additional paintings of Washington.

CHAPTER 8

Paying for Peace

As 1793 came to an end, Jefferson resigned as secretary of state, retiring to Monticello to consider his future. In the year after his departure, the United States managed to reach a peace agreement with Hassan, the dey of Algiers—a deal meaning that, against Jefferson's advice, Americans would pay for peace, including the release of prisoners. Though there was no longer any immediate need for more naval ships, President Washington did persuade Congress that stopping the shipbuilding would be unwise.

Washington's instincts proved sound. Because the Americans were perennially slow in making their payments, the dey threatened war and refused to release the prisoners until he was paid. The Americans were relieved that they had kept the shipbuilding going, and the USS *United States*, USS *Constellation*, and USS *Constitution* launched in 1797.

By 1797, Joel Barlow, a patriot of the Revolution and a diplomat, was on duty as ambassador to the volatile leader of Algiers. President Washington had dispatched him the previous year to "take charge of the interests of the United States of America within the Regency of Algiers." His goal was to maintain the peace—and gain the release of Richard O'Brien and his men.

Barlow was clearly equipped for the difficult diplomacy needed in Algiers; he seemed like a man who could deal with whatever came his way. He had the brains, the courage, and the courtly manner to be an expert diplomat, but it wasn't clear that these qualities would be enough to rescue the American slaves.

The three-masted frigate USS Constitution *(right) was the third ship built for the new Navy. She is heavier and carries more cannon than other frigates built at the time.*

Joel Barlow, created in 1793

When Barlow arrived as American consul to Algiers, he was confronted with the dey's refusal to release the prisoners until the United States fulfilled its monetary promises. Barlow gave his word that payment was forthcoming and, in the meantime, plied the Algerian ruler with diamond rings, brocade robes, carpets, jeweled snuffboxes, and other goods he had brought with him, treasures worth more than $27,000. Some mix of personality, placating gifts, and promises of money persuaded the dey, who—at last—released the prisoners. Their ranks had been reduced by harsh prison conditions and illness, but Barlow guided eighty-five survivors aboard the ship *Fortune*, and watched them depart for friendlier shores.

After O'Brien and the other captives went free, Barlow and his fellow American consuls in the region remained behind to finish a series of impossibly complicated negotiations. Committed to purchasing a treaty, in accordance with newly elected president John Adams's wishes, Barlow put up with diplomatic tricks, delays, broken promises, and shaky deals. Bowing to the Algerians' humiliating demands, the American government would agree to hand over money and goods worth close to a million dollars, a cost equal to one-eighth of the federal government's annual expenditures.

The Treaty of Peace and Friendship between the United States and Tripoli was signed in November 1796. It included the usual provisions, one for payment of tribute and another for the delivery of maritime and military supplies, in return for free passage of American ships and mutual cooperation.

The treaty was ratified by the United States Congress in June 1797, and Barlow returned to France, having spent only two years in North Africa but leaving two new treaties in place. Two more—with the remaining Barbary States, Morocco and Tunis—would shortly be signed. Between the treaties and the freeing of the long-imprisoned sailors, Barlow's brief tenure had been a success.

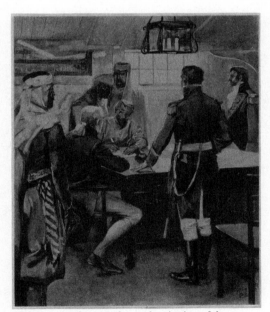

This imagined scene shows the signing of the peace treaty between the United States and the dey of Algiers on January 3, 1797.

Part

Two

CHAPTER 9

Jefferson Takes Charge

In 1800, Thomas Jefferson, then vice president in John Adams's administration, decided to run for president. After a bitter contest that threatened the unity of the new nation, he won the election against John Adams, his friend and the sitting president, and was inaugurated on March 4, 1801, as the third president of the United States.

Unaware that the ticking time bomb of the Barbary Coast was about to go off, Jefferson settled gradually into his new home. After his walk to the Capitol building in Washington, D.C., for his inauguration, he let two full weeks pass before moving from his rented rooms into the still-unfinished president's quarters.

President Jefferson ordered that all official correspondence be submitted to him for review. As he looked over the papers Adams had left behind, his concern about America's safety grew. Jefferson had known the Barbary situation was bad, but he hadn't realized

James Cathcart

how bad it truly was until he reviewed the existing treaties with Algiers, Tripoli, and Tunis. The last had been ratified in January 1800 and promised payment of $20,000 in annual tribute. After fifteen years of observation, Jefferson knew as well as anyone that this demand had not been made in good faith. Instead, it was a warning that the whole region was nothing less than a powder keg.

The U.S. representatives along the Barbary Coast were Richard O'Brien, the former captain of the *Dauphin* and ten-year captive, now consul general to the Barbary States; James Cathcart, also a former prisoner, now consul to Tripoli; and William Eaton, consul general to Tunis.

On March 13, another stack of dispatches from the Mediterranean arrived for Jefferson's review. One dated October 1800 from James Cathcart, who was serving as special agent to William Eaton, was particularly alarming. Cathcart reported that the bashaw, or ruler, of Tripoli had demanded an increase in his annual tribute, despite the provision in the treaty stating that no "periodical tribute or farther payment is ever to be made by either party." That provision, Cathcart reported, was of no importance whatever to the ruler.

As Jefferson read on, Cathcart's long and detailed letter grew more ominous. The bashaw's language had turned to explicit threats.

"Let your government give me a sum of money & I will be content—but I will be paid one way or the other." The bashaw set a six-month deadline; if his demands were not met by then, he said, "I will declare war . . . against the United States." Those six months were nearly up.

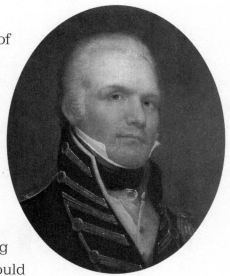

William Eaton

Jefferson also found a letter from Tunis consul William Eaton. Sensing that the fragile peace with Tunis would not last, Eaton had begged Adams's administration to make a show of strength. He proposed sending three of America's largest fighting ships into Tripoli. There he would invite the bashaw to dinner and impress him with the Americans' strength. After the meal, he would point at the cannon and say, "See there our executive power Commissioned to Keep Guarentee of Peace." If the plan worked, Eaton explained, the bashaw might be too intimidated to declare war.

Unfortunately, one of former president Adams's last acts in office had been to sign into law a bill shrinking the American navy. Jefferson sympathized with Eaton, whose plan resembled Jefferson's own from years earlier, but there were few ships to send. These vessels were slow to build, and Jefferson did not have enough military power to take America properly to war.

A plan was taking shape in Jefferson's mind—a plan that would fall somewhere between submitting to the Barbary indignities and launching a full-scale war. Jefferson needed to convene his cabinet to secure their approval. He had hoped to gather his cabinet in Washington by the end of April, but it was mid-May before they assembled.

The situation on the Barbary Coast demanded action, even though everyone at the table also understood that the United States was among the least qualified of nations to take on pirates with its small navy, which was shrinking further even as they took their seats.

Jefferson put the question boldly, asking his advisers at this, his first cabinet meeting, "Shall the squadron now at Norfolk be ordered to cruise in the Mediterranean?"

Richard Dale

After further discussion, the cabinet was unanimous: the squadron would be dispatched to the Mediterranean, but as peacemakers rather than agents of war. Jefferson and his cabinet hoped against hope that the Barbary powers would be reasonable, would recognize that the United States took seriously the seizure of its goods and citizens, and would back down from the conflict.

Richard Dale, one of the original U.S. Navy captains appointed by George Washington, was named to command the squadron. He would carry with him a letter from President Jefferson, addressed to the leader of Tripoli; in its text, Jefferson offered multiple assurances of constant friendship.

Jefferson chose his words carefully, avoiding inflammatory terms such as "warship" to keep the tone civil. He advised the bashaw that he had detached a squadron as observers in the Mediterranean.

President Jefferson could only hope that his words of peace, accompanied by a modest show of power, would quiet the visions of war that danced in the mind of Yusuf Qaramanli, the bashaw of Tripoli.

CHAPTER 10

War

While Jefferson and his cabinet prepared a response to Barbary provocation, James Cathcart stood in a diplomatic no-man's-land. For almost six months he had waited impatiently for a response from his government to his letter outlining the war threats from Tripolitan bashaw Yusuf Qaramanli. No instructions came. He didn't even know who had won the presidential election. For all intents and purposes, Cathcart was alone.

Over the past few months, the bashaw had alternately threatened and flattered the United States. He had told Cathcart he wanted peace with the American people, but refused to discuss the existing treaty, still legally in effect. The bashaw simply wanted more than he had agreed to in the past and didn't pretend otherwise. He first demanded a gift of ships—the other regencies had gotten more in their treaties, he pointed out, Algiers in particular. Now he insisted upon further considerations, too. The bashaw demanded immense amounts of money, including a down payment of $225,000, far more than Cathcart could give or the U.S. Treasury could afford. The bashaw was shameless in his demands, and even had the audacity to press for an additional $10,000 in tribute when George Washington died.

His fear rising, Cathcart had issued a circular letter to his fellow consuls on February 21, 1801. "I am convinced that the Bashaw of Tripoli," he warned, "will commence Hostilitys against the U. States of America in less than Sixty Days."

He was not far off; his fears were confirmed on May 11, 1801, three months later.

At six o'clock that Monday evening, a representative from the bashaw arrived at the American consulate in Tripoli. When the visitor was ushered in, Cathcart immediately recognized the man as one of Bashaw Yusuf's most esteemed advisers. Cathcart greeted him with all the cordiality he could muster. He had done his best to remain patient with the bashaw's games, but his patience with the constant demands was wearing thin.

This time, the bashaw's emissary didn't even pretend to come in peace. He delivered his message: "The Bashaw has sent me to inform you that he has declared war against the United States and will take down your flagstaff on Thursday the 14th."

The bashaw had made many threats in the past, but Cathcart understood this one was real. Cathcart replied politely to the bashaw's emissary, knowing that an angry reply would only jeopardize his wife and young daughter, who resided with him, as well as his diplomatic staff. Without instructions from the government at home, he was authorized to do nothing else. And even if he could know the new president's mind, military backup would never reach him in time. Accordingly, Cathcart acknowledged receipt of the declaration of war and said he would charter a ship and depart the city as soon as possible. In the meantime, he remained at the consulate and witnessed the first official act of war.

Three days later, the bashaw made good on his threat. The bashaw's soldiers arrived at the American consulate. They shouted encouragement to one another as they swung their axes, but felling the flagpole was harder than they had expected. Chips flew, but the flagpole refused to fall. As if to mock the men, the flag fluttered with each stroke of the axes, its staff staunchly in place. A gesture meant to humble the Americans was rapidly becoming a humiliation for the Tripolitans.

The bashaw had ordered that if the men had trouble dropping the pole, they should pull on the halyard, the line anchored at the top of the pole used to hoist the flag. He thought they might be able to break the pole in half by doing so. To the dismay of the men, that strategy failed, too, and once again, the resilient flagpole refused to fall.

More than an hour passed before the Tripolitans finally caused the pole to splinter just enough to lean against the consulate house. The American diplomats looked on, darkly amused by the whole episode. Cathcart wryly recorded the events in a dispatch to Secretary of State James Madison.

"At a quarter past two they effected the grand atchievement and our Flagstaff was chop'd down six feet from the ground &

left reclining on the Terrace. . . . Thus ends the first act of this Tragedy."

Ten days would pass before Cathcart, his wife, and his daughter sailed out of Tripoli harbor aboard a polacca, a small three-masted ship he hired in the harbor. He entrusted the consulate affairs he left behind to the good hands of the Danish consul general, Nicholas Nissen. Cathcart specifically instructed that any American sailors

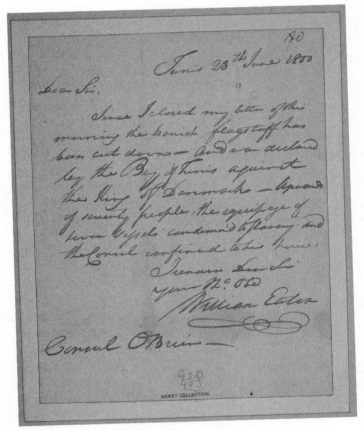

William Eaton's letter to Consul O'Brien describing the destruction of the flagstaff. "The Danish flagstaff has been cut down, and war declared by the Bey of Tunis against Denmark; seventy people, the equipage of seven vessels, are condemned to slavery, and the consul confined to his house."

brought captive to Tripoli be provided for with money for food and needed medical care. Nissen agreed to do whatever was in his power to meet those needs should another American ship be captured.

Once they were ashore in Italy, the news finally reached Cathcart of Jefferson's election. He sent his congratulations, via a letter to Madison, who along with Jefferson would remain unaware for many more weeks that Tripoli had declared war. Jefferson would learn of Tripoli's attack too late to assist Cathcart, who was already traveling home. But thanks to Jefferson's foresight, American ships had already been ordered to head for the Barbary Coast. They were not authorized to attack the Barbary ships, but they would be able to defend American interests against further embarrassment and blockade Barbary ports, squeezing Tripoli's economy the same way the pirates had been squeezing America's. Both nations knew that a breaking point had been reached, but neither side knew that the other had taken action.

CHAPTER 11

The First Flotilla

An ocean away from Cathcart's splintered flagpole, Jefferson's four warships prepared for their voyage. The flagship would be the frigate USS *President*, commanded by Commodore Richard Dale. The *Philadelphia* and the *Essex*, captained by Samuel Barron and William Bainbridge, respectively, would add additional strength. A fourth vessel, the trim schooner *Enterprise*, guided by Lieutenant Andrew Sterett, completed the flotilla. Though modest in numbers, the flotilla was surprisingly powerful due to a new design. Because of innovations in American shipbuilding, the American frigates would be able to outrun much larger ships or, in heavy seas, match up with them.

William Bainbridge

Adding to the military might of the four

Building the USS Philadelphia *in a shipyard in Philadelphia.*

ships were members of the relatively new United States Marine Corps, reactivated by President Adams with the birth of the U.S. Navy in 1798. Skilled combatants, the Marines were invaluable during boarding actions and landing expeditions, and they also served to protect a ship's officers in the event of a mutiny by the crew. The fighters had a reputation for being bold, fearless men—though sometimes a little brash and reckless. Their presence would be beneficial should any of Dale's ships encounter pirates or his men need protection on land.

Once fully provisioned, Dale's squadron finally made sail for the Strait of Gibraltar on June 2, 1801. Soon after losing sight of the American coast, they met with rough seas. Swirling squalls made the first ten days of the crossing difficult, as easterly winds and heavy rains buffeted the ships. As the newest of the four American vessels, the USS *President* had only a few months of sailing to her credit, and the storms found every flaw in her construction. Wracked by the thrashing of the sea, she soon had rain and seawater leaking through seams that opened in her deck. Life below became damp and unpleasant, and many of the crew were seasick. But she was a fine ship, from the top of her three tall masts to her bottom. A little stormy weather would not prevent the USS *President* from reaching her Mediterranean destination.

When Dale's ships emerged from the gales, the commodore began running his men through cannon drills. Each man had a precise role in the exercises, and soon the air was filled with orders

PRESIDENT AND PLANTAGENET.

The USS President *in the foreground.*

to fire. With a deafening roar, cannonball shot flew hundreds of yards before disappearing into the waves.

During the voyage, the captains trained their men, veteran and novice alike, for a kind of warfare particular to the Barbary Coast. There would be no lines of battle, with opposing enemy fleets facing off. When attacking, Barbary ships closed rapidly, their first strategy to board their opponent. Smaller than the U.S. ships, the pirate ships approached quickly, sailing up to the sides of the frigates. Barbary sailors would leap onto ships and swarm the crew. Thus the best defense for a ship under Barbary attack was coordinated cannon fire to keep the pirates at a distance.

To Dale's frustration, though, a good defense was all he was authorized to do. Beginning with the debate in his cabinet in Washington two and a half months before, President Jefferson hesitated to claim with certainty that he had the constitutional right to declare war. Thus, the orders transmitted down the line of command—via the secretary of the navy, to Commodore Dale, and on to his captains—were abundantly clear. "Should you fall in with any of the Tripolitan Corsairs . . . on your passage to Malta," Dale wrote, ". . . you will heave all his Guns Over board[,] Cut away his Masts, & leave him In a situation, that he can Just make out to get into some Port." American ships were not to capture any Barbary ships. They could hobble ships that attacked them, but they were to take no captives and let their enemies escape.

CHAPTER 12

To Algiers and Tunis

Even if they were not authorized for full-on war, the four American ships, Jefferson hoped, would win new respect for the United States of America. The armada's guns were impressive, and its captains brave, but whether four ships would impress the pirates remained to be seen. And whether the Barbary States would peacefully back down before a modest show of force was an even more important question.

When the *President* and *Enterprise* rode the tide into Algiers harbor on July 9, a delighted Richard O'Brien greeted his fellow Americans. He then delivered a letter to the dey on Dale's behalf, a letter designed to offer "the Profound respect which is due to your Excellency's dignity and character." The note also explained the mission in subtle but clear terms: these ships would "superintend the safety of [American] Commerce." It was lost on no one who saw the U.S. Navy vessels that these guardians were armed with many guns, but Dale was careful to make no threats.

Two days later, the two ships weighed anchor and set out for Tunis, where Commodore Dale would first meet William Eaton, consul to Tunis and a man who shared Dale's feeling that the United States must fight, not pay.

Predictably, the Tunisians responded to Dale's greetings with many demands. A few months before, the new dey of Algiers, Bobba Mustapha, had written to the president asking for forty twenty-four-pound guns and forty other pieces. He also wanted ten thousand rifles. Dale could do little but add his promises that the "regalia due to him" was on its way. Fortunately, his words soon proved true with the arrival in Tunis the following day of a merchant ship carrying the tribute, escorted by the USS *Essex*.

Along with Eaton, Dale found his patience dwindling. Dale needed more ships—and the authorization to use them in battle—if he was going to get anywhere.

CHAPTER 13

To Tripoli

With little return for his diplomacy thus far, Dale headed to Tripoli, where he would encounter the most difficult leader of all. Dale hoped to resolve matters with the Tripolitans. If he could not, this time he would be authorized by Jefferson to use force to contain the enemy because they had declared war on the United States.

The USS *President* and USS *Enterprise* reached Tripoli harbor on July 24, 1801. Beyond the coastal reefs and shoals, the American ships patrolled, seeking to control access to the channels leading to Tripoli's inner harbor.

Though he could not freely walk its streets, Commodore Dale knew that this port city of some thirty thousand citizens was suffering. Tripoli was already partially blockaded by ships from Sweden's Royal Navy, as the belligerent Bashaw Yusuf was at odds with that nation, too. Most of the people were without grain and other basic foodstuffs. Dale hoped that his additional blockade, should it become necessary, would hasten the humbling of the bashaw.

On Saturday, July 25, Dale ordered a letter delivered to the bashaw. The letter was long, couched in the best diplomatic terms that Dale could muster. He began by expressing his disappointment at the bashaw's declaration of war against the United States, then followed with fair warning: "I am sorry to Inform Your Excellency—that your Conduct towards the President of the United States, In declaring war against him, has put me under the necessity of Commencing hostilities against your Excellency's Vessels and subjects, where ever I may fall in with them."

But Dale closed his message on a conciliatory note: if the bashaw had any wish to withdraw his declaration of war and make peace, he might send a delegation by boat to the *President*, where Dale would be eager to receive them.

Sunday passed with no response.

On Monday, a boat approached the *President* asking that a messenger carrying the bashaw's response be taken on board. Eager for an answer, Dale granted the request, and the Americans helped the messenger aboard.

The response was given: the bashaw declared, quite simply, that he had not declared war without provocation. No further explanation was offered.

Dale composed another letter, attempting to move the conversation forward. He dispatched it the following day, on Tuesday, July 28.

This time silence spoke for the bashaw.

If he had not been certain before, Dale now knew the time for diplomatic dodges and niceties had passed, but he wanted to make sure military engagements happened on his own terms. The bashaw's navy was small. The American navy would be able to take on the Barbary forces in the open sea, but attempting to bombard the harbor was a different matter. Because Commodore Dale and his captains lacked charts of the unfamiliar harbor, the many reefs and rocks posed a grave danger. Dale decided the wisest course was to blockade the harbor and hope for a chance to engage with enemy ships venturing in or out.

No ships emerged from the harbor in the days that followed. With the unforgiving July sun, the water rations aboard the *President* and *Enterprise* soon ran low. Replenishing supplies meant a trip to the nearest safe harbor, at Malta, several days' sail away. Dale didn't want to lose one of his ships for the week or more needed for the journey, but he had no choice. On July 30, Dale sent the *Enterprise* off, its orders "to take in as much water as you can possibley bring back." Now on its own, the *President* would maintain its watch off the shoals of Tripoli.

CHAPTER 14

The First Shots of the War

The USS *Enterprise* made sail for Malta to procure much-needed water. But Lieutenant Andrew Sterett's simple errand was about to be interrupted.

On August 1, the second day out, and less than an hour into the morning watch, a lookout spied a ship at the horizon. Suspecting it was part of Bashaw Yusuf's navy, Sterett ordered his men to prepare for battle.

On this day, the *Enterprise* flew a British flag, a deception permitted by Dale's orders. Because Tripoli and Great Britain were at peace, the enemy ship's captain made no move to flee as a ship that appeared to be British approached.

The ships slowed, coming along-

Andrew Sterett

side each other at shouting distance. Sterett hailed the captain, asking the object of his cruise.

Thinking he had no quarrel with this ship, the master of the *Tripoli* spoke the truth. He had come to find the Americans. Before Sterett could reply, the Tripolitan captain complained that he had yet to find any Americans to fight.

Acting instantly, Sterett ordered the British flag lowered, as Dale had ordered him to engage in combat only while flying the American flag. As the U.S. colors went up the pole, Sterett in full voice issued the order to fire. The crackle of muskets filled the air.

The Tripolitans returned scattered fire. The first shots of the war rang out over the water.

Within moments, the American guns produced a deafening roar. Along with the flying cannonballs, streaks of lightning seemed to emerge from the iron cannon muzzles. The crashing sound of solid shot striking the *Tripoli* followed a heartbeat later. At such close range, few shots missed their mark.

Aboard the Tripolitan ship, masts splintered, crashing to the deck. The rigging sagged, and ropes whipped back and forth as the ship rocked; holes appeared in the ship's hull above the waterline.

Their first volley over, the American gunners raced to reload, swabbing, ramming, and firing again. The well-drilled men hit most of their targets.

The fight between the USS Enterprise (left) and the Tripoli *(right).*

The enemy ship's cables and anchors went into the sea. Unaccustomed to relying entirely upon artillery, Admiral Mahomet Rous of the *Tripoli* ordered his men to maneuver their vessel alongside the *Enterprise*. They would board this American adversary and swarm over her sides, knives and pistols in hand. They would fight as they preferred: hand-to-hand, man-to-man. That was the pirate way.

But the small Marine Corps detachment aboard the *Enterprise* was ready. At the order of Marine Lieutenant Enoch Lane, their deadly musket fire repulsed the approaching pirates, dropping many to the decks before they even had a chance to swing their swords.

The *Tripoli* moved off, and seeming to surrender, the Tripolitans lowered their flag. Seeing this signal, the men of the *Enterprise* naively assembled on deck and let loose the traditional three cheers as a mark of victory. Within moments, the cheers were drowned out by the sound of gunfire. The pirates, disregarding the rules of war, had raised their flag again and were firing on the exposed Americans, who ran to their stations.

The battle quickly resumed, and the hellish American fire brought the Tripolitans to surrender a second time, and then a third, only to see the enemy's flag twice lower and rise again.

Finally, seething at this treachery, Sterett ordered his gunners to fire until they were sure the *Tripoli* would sink beneath the waves. The cry of "Sink the Villains!" echoed aboard the *Enterprise*. In the long minutes that followed, the pirates' fire grew progressively weaker, but the sustained American cannonade did not cease until the admiral called for mercy. Three hours after the first shot was fired, the wounded Rous, standing at his ship's gunwale, bowed

Cannon smoke often obscured the enemy target.

deeply in genuine supplication and surrender. This time he threw his flag into the sea.

The silence that ensued was broken not by gunfire, but only by the moans of the wounded.

Rous could not be rowed to the *Enterprise* to offer his sword to Sterett, the traditional act of conceding victory; the *Tripoli*'s harbor boat was no longer seaworthy, shattered by the cannon fire. Lieutenant Sterett, after receiving assurances as to their safety, dispatched a group of his officers and seamen in the *Enterprise*'s boat. When the Americans boarded the enemy's vessel, they saw a scene of terrible carnage. Thirty men had been killed and another thirty wounded. Bodies lay in pools of blood, as rivulets of red poured through the ship's hatches.

An amazed Sterett found that in comparison with the slaughter aboard the *Tripoli*, the Americans had sustained no casualties, with no one either killed or injured. He ordered his surgeon to minister to the enemy wounded, as the Tripolitan surgeon was among the dead.

Admiral Rous's ship was in perilous condition. Her sails and rigging had been cut to pieces; one of her three masts teetered precariously before crashing over the side. Solid shot had torn eighteen holes in the hull of the *Tripoli* above the waterline.

Lieutenant Andrew Sterett leaves the USS Enterprise *on the way to board the* Tripoli.

Under other circumstances, the *Tripoli* would have been regarded as fairly won and Lieutenant Sterett would have put a crew of his own men aboard to sail her to port as the spoils of victory. But Sterett, a stickler for procedure, honored his orders not to take captives.

Instead of commandeering the ship, Sterett's men set about incapacitating it. Cannons, powder, cannonballs, swords, and small arms went into the sea, along with the ship's cables and anchors. After chopping down the ship's remaining masts, the victors raised a spar affixed with a tattered sail—just enough to move the boat along. Leaving the defeated *Tripoli* to limp home, the *Enterprise* continued on her way to Malta.

Several days later, on August 6, the crew of the frigate *President* spotted Sterett's battle-scarred victims approaching Tripoli harbor. Maintaining the blockade, Dale stopped the ship and questioned its crew. Anxious to get home, the captain of the *Tripoli* insisted that they were Tunisians headed to Malta who had been attacked by a French ship. Thinking the tale plausible, Commodore Dale lent the captain a compass "& Suffer'd him to proceed on" into Tripoli harbor. The enemy ship had escaped, but only after embarrassing losses.

CHAPTER 15

The News Reaches America

With the slow transmission of news across the Atlantic, Americans did not learn what had happened off Malta until two months later. But on November 11, 1801, the editors of the *National Intelligencer*, a Washington, D.C., newspaper, described proudly the stunning victory of the USS *Enterprise*. Thrilled by the American triumph, Congress voted to commission a commemorative sword for Sterett and awarded his officers and crewmen an extra month's pay.

To Jefferson, the dramatic vanquishing of the *Tripoli* in the hard-fought, three-hour sea battle sounded like political leverage. On December 8, he proudly cited the bravery of Lieutenant Sterett and the men aboard the USS *Enterprise* in his annual presidential message. "After a heavy slaughter of [enemy] men," Jefferson told Congress, the U.S. Navy ship had prevailed "without the loss of a single one on our part."

The encouragement brought by Sterett's victory came none too soon. America had been dealing with the Barbary pirates for years with few results. Appeasement had not worked: poor Cathcart had suffered the results of that tactic when he was forced to flee the consulate. Richard Dale's diplomacy tour had been ineffective: his blockade had let an enemy ship through. The only effective action so far had been the use of focused military power in the face of a threat.

Jefferson was no warmonger. He had attempted to keep the peace despite his instincts. But now he felt justified in calling for America to go to war. It was about time. The Barbary States were already at war with America, and they seemed to understand only one kind of diplomacy: the kind that was accompanied by a cannon.

The bombing of Tripoli by the famous American printer Currier & Ives.

CHAPTER 16

Richard Dale Returns Home

Richard Dale was forced to abandon Tripoli on September 3, 1801. Though his ships had replenished their supply of water, thanks to Sterett, the lack of fresh food on board had taken a toll, as more than 150 members of his crew were down with a "kind of Enfluenza." In October, Dale learned that his tour of duty—mandated by Congress to be just one year—would not be extended. He and the *President* began their journey home. It was not an easy journey: the ship ran aground in the narrow Gibraltar passage, underwent three days of heavy gales, and had to take refuge in Toulon, France, for repairs. Finally, on April 14, 1802, the *President* returned to port.

CHAPTER  17

A New Plan Is Developing

Jefferson appeared to be waiting passively for Congress to act. In reality, he was hatching a clandestine plan. This one was not for the pages of the *National Intelligencer* or the ears of Congress. This plan would not just persuade the Barbary States to stop harassing Americans; it would instead change the rulers of those states. So far it was little more than an idea, but that idea had begun to grow.

U.S. consul William Eaton had written to Secretary of State James Madison, hoping that a strategy that went beyond using frigates might meet with sympathetic ears. Eaton had learned from James Cathcart, the U.S. consul to Tripoli, that Bashaw Yusuf had no legal right to lead Tripoli. Hamet Qaramanli, his brother, was the rightful heir to the throne. Yusuf had stolen the throne by murdering his oldest brother; Hamet, next in line, had been banished by Yusuf and now lived in exile, pining for his wife and four children, whom his brother kept as hostages in Tripoli. Eaton had a wild proposal. In a

James Madison

dispatch home, Eaton proposed to Madison that the Americans ally themselves with the bashaw's exiled brother.

Eaton had met Hamet briefly when Hamet had stopped in Tunis after his banishment. The two men had shared a meal of lamb and vegetables and discussed the best way to deal with the dangerous new bashaw. In the plan they concocted, the American consul had seen a chance both to right Hamet's personal injustices and to solve America's problems once and for all.

For this venture, Captain Eaton planned to abandon his consul's garb and don his military uniform. He wrote to Madison that he wanted "to attack the usurper by land, while our operations are going on by sea." It would be a military mission, with the goal of revolution in Tripoli: the overthrow of Yusuf and nothing less than the restoration of Hamet to the throne.

Even if the idea seemed outlandish at first, Madison and Jefferson realized they had to take Eaton seriously. In his years in Tunis, Eaton's skill with languages had enabled him to master several Arabic dialects, and he had gained intimate knowledge of the Barbary Coast and its people. Eaton knew the traditions of North Africa as well as any foreigner could. When he reported that "the subjects in general of the reigning Bashaw are very discontented, and ripe for revolt," he spoke from firsthand knowledge. He offered assurances that the United States would not be the only government supporting such an effort: "The Bey of Tunis, though prudence will keep him behind the curtain, I have strong reason to believe, will cheerfully promote the scheme."

For years Consul Eaton had been making a persuasive case for sending ships to the Mediterranean. He had called for force, and he had been right. Jefferson knew he had to listen to this new idea, but there was no denying that it was a daring departure from earlier strategies, so he was determined to act prudently and wait for the right moment.

As 1801 ended, Jefferson and Madison conducted business as usual in the nation's capital, publicly looking to get formal authorization for the force needed to widen the blockade. The other plan, the secret plan, was still just an idea, a future option. And far away, on a Mediterranean shore, William Eaton and Hamet, the rightful bashaw, carried on their conversation.

CHAPTER 18

An Act of Protection

On February 6, 1802, President Jefferson got his wish when the Senate approved the use of force along the Barbary Coast, if Jefferson deemed it necessary. Brandishing his pen, he signed into law "An Act for the protection of the Commerce and Seamen of the United States, against Tripolitan Corsairs."

Though it was less than a declaration of war, the legislation spoke without ambiguity. Hereafter, as set forth in the act, "it shall be lawful fully to equip, officer, man, and employ such of the armed vessels of the United States as may be judged requisite by the President of the United States, for protecting effectually the commerce and seamen thereof on the Atlantic ocean, the Mediterranean and adjoining seas." Jefferson could now send as many ships as he needed to North Africa, and they could do whatever it took to keep American ships safe. Mr. Jefferson's navy could now pursue the Tripolitan pirates as he saw fit.

Although President Jefferson had been shaping a strategy for years, he depended on the opinion of his consuls at the front more than on his own judgment. Several of these men had asked for added military might, but Richard O'Brien, writing to James Madison in mid-1801, put the case plainly: "I am convinced that Tripoli should have . . . [cannon] Balls without delay. We want sir 3—or 6—or more of our frigates in this sea."

Now that Jefferson was free to act, he honored O'Brien's request, ordering an increase in the size of the American naval force in early 1802. The ship designated as the fleet's flagship was the USS *Chesapeake*. The frigate would join the USS *Philadelphia*, which,

USS Chesapeake *after the First Barbary War.*

along with the USS *Essex*, remained in the Mediterranean, escorting merchant ships. Two other frigates would sail from Norfolk that spring, the USS *Constellation* and the USS *Adams*. On returning from the Mediterranean, the master of the sloop *Enterprise*, Lieutenant Sterett, was to turn his ship around again and recross the Atlantic to join the five frigates.

With the new fleet assembling, Jefferson finally had the firepower and the authorization to defend American interests. Intimidating the pirates would be easier than getting involved in their government, and if all went well, there would be no need to secretly plan a coup. Jefferson anticipated a quick and tidy ending to the years of conflict, but he had made one key mistake: he'd appointed the wrong man to lead the new force.

CHAPTER 19

The Wrong Man

Captain Richard Valentine Morris was the president's choice for commander of the new flotilla. A victor in several sea battles in an undeclared war against France that lasted from 1798–1800, Richard Morris was a bold young officer who accepted the assignment eagerly. But the thirty-four-year-old captain's marital status had changed since his service in the Caribbean—and it was Mrs. Morris who submitted an unusual appeal regarding her husband's terms of deployment. Writing directly to the secretary of the navy, she asked permission to sail with her husband.

The request was not without precedent, but it was rare for a wife to travel on her husband's ship in a time of war. Nevertheless, the secretary immediately granted it, and when Captain Morris came aboard the *Chesapeake* he was accompanied not only by his wife but also by their young son. It isn't precisely clear what the sailors thought of the family's presence, but soon it became apparent that the captain's mind was not on his job.

The secretary of the navy wanted an American show of force off Tripoli as soon as possible, so the six ships sailed not as a convoy but as soon as their individual preparations permitted. The *Chesapeake* arrived in Gibraltar on May 25, requiring some repairs to her mast. But that proved no hardship for Morris and his wife, who soon settled into the busy social life of the British port, dining with the new governor of Gibraltar and hobnobbing with British royalty. The English officers and their wives welcomed both the commodore and the "Commodoress," as Mrs. Morris

The Rock of Gibraltar is a limestone outcropping overlooking Gibraltar harbor. At the time, Gibraltar was a British territory. This drawing imagines a battle in the harbor.

came to be known. Meanwhile, disgruntled American sailors found themselves sentenced to remain in port for weeks, which stretched into months. They were stuck swabbing the decks, sewing their sails, and waiting while their captain feasted with foreign aristocrats.

When the USS *Adams*, far behind her sister ships, arrived in Gibraltar on July 21, 1802, her captain found Morris's *Chesapeake* still at anchor, though her mast was repaired and she was fully seaworthy. The Morris family was enjoying the high life in the port city and seemed to have no desire to move on to war.

The *Adams* carried orders from the secretary of the navy for the lazy commodore. Now three months old, the instructions were clear and specific. Morris was to take his entire naval force to Tripoli. The hope was that "holding out the olive Branch in one hand & displaying in the other the means of offensive operations [will] produce a peaceful disposition toward us in the mind of the Bashaw, and essentially to contribute to our obtaining an advantageous treat with him." The flotilla was to make the case for peace even as it threatened military action.

On August 17, Morris finally left Gibraltar, but still chose not to do as instructed. He made no strong military show off Tripoli, but instead cruised the southern European coast, making stops at friendly ports. At one port he found Captain Murray and the USS *Constellation*, which had left Tripoli in need of both water and repairs. That meant the ineffective American blockade had officially ceased. Far from Tripoli, Morris wrote his first report in several months to the secretary of the navy. Morris would make no effort to reestablish a naval presence in enemy waters; because of the "advanced period of the season," he explained, it would be "impossible to appear off Tripoli before January." The Tripolitan pirates had little to fear that winter.

CHAPTER 20

A Last Chance

It had been nearly a year since the *Chesapeake* left Norfolk. Due for a regular refitting, it returned to the United States, and Morris took command of a new flagship, the USS *New York*.

On April 25, 1803, after eleven months in the Mediterranean, Morris saw Tripoli for the first time. But it was a short visit. There was an explosion on board that resulted in the death of crew members and severe burns to others. The USS *New York* retuned to Malta for repairs, and Morris's blockade of Tripoli was delayed yet again.

Finally, on May 22, 1803, Morris began a five-week exercise in the enemy harbor. By then it was too late. Having exasperated his superiors, he was relieved of his command.

The letter addressed to him from the secretary of the navy was unambiguous: "You will upon receipt of this consider yourself Suspended in the command of the Squadron on the Mediterranean Station."

William Eaton, having returned to Washington in the late spring, had duly reported on Morris's inactivity. By Eaton's count, Morris had been off the coast of Tripoli a total of only nineteen days in the course of his seventeen-month tour of duty.

Given his lackluster performance, he would be required to face a court-martial. The trial lasted for nine days. After due deliberation, the four-man panel determined that "captain Morris did not conduct himself, in his command of the Mediterranean squadron, with the diligence or activity necessary." His bravery was not questioned; his fault, the panel ruled, lay in "his indolence, and want of capacity." He was immediately dismissed from the U.S. Navy.

CHAPTER 21

Time for a Man of Action

Appalled at how poorly Morris had performed, Jefferson took great care in appointing his next commander. He needed a man with both diplomatic tact and courage, a leader who would take initiative and press for his country's best interests. Jefferson's patience with both the pirates and incompetent American leadership had worn thin. It was time for action, so he would appoint a man of action: Edward Preble. At age forty, Edward Preble had spent more of his years at sea than on land. At sixteen, after announcing to his father that he had hoed his last row of potatoes, he had shipped out on a privateer he spotted in the harbor. From then on he was a man of the sea.

At the command of the USS *Con-*

Edward Preble

Tobias Lear

stitution, he set out from Boston Harbor on August 12, 1803. His principal passengers were Colonel and Mrs. Tobias Lear. The colonel was President Jefferson's new appointee to the post of consul general at Algiers following Richard O'Brien's retirement. Just days before the *Constitution* sailed, the secretary of the navy had advised Preble, "Your experience in affairs and your good sense and the tried merits of Mr. Lear all conspire to persuade me that you and he will move in the most perfect harmony." The man of war and the seeker of treaties had become collaborators. It was their task to sort out the mess, militarily and diplomatically. They were to do, in short, whatever it took along the Barbary Coast. They spent the transatlantic voyage planning accordingly.

A surprise awaited Preble and Lear at the Bay of Gibraltar. William Bainbridge, whose ship, the USS *Philadelphia*, was anchored in Gibraltar, informed Preble that Tripoli wasn't their only sworn enemy. After confronting a strange ship at sea, Bainbridge had discovered that it carried a kidnapped American crew and orders from the sultan of Morocco to capture American ships, their crew, and their cargo. With Morocco joining Algiers and Tripoli in the hostilities, Tunis was the only Barbary state not at war with the Americans, and even that peace looked shaky.

CHAPTER 22

A Show of Force at Morocco

After deliberations with Lear, Preble decided to proceed on two fronts. First, Preble and most of his squadron would present a great show of force at Morocco. He didn't want to expand the war—he could hardly attack Tripoli if his forces were badly divided—but he couldn't afford to ignore this new antagonist, either. He wanted his Moroccan challengers to think he was spoiling for a fight; that might lead to a quick settlement, which would free him up to focus his energies on the threats posed elsewhere in the region. Like President Jefferson, he was convinced that "nothing will keep the [villains] so quiet as a respectable naval force near them." If a show of power was required, he was there to provide it.

Second, Bainbridge would take the *Philadelphia* to Tripoli, escorting U.S. merchant ships along the way, attacking any pirate ships they encountered and capturing their crew.

When the sultan of Morocco, Maulay Sulaiman, finally returned

Bainbridge meets the dey of Algiers in September 1800.

from a journey two weeks later, the full force of the U.S. Navy was on display in Tangier harbor. Before the sultan's eyes was an intimidating display of raw naval power; the American guns, numbering well over 150 cannons, could likely pound the city's crumbling stone castle and sink every vessel in the harbor.

Preble maintained a commanding position looking in on Tangier harbor, well outside the range of the sultan's cannons.

Preble exchanged letters with Maulay Sulaiman. The two men agreed upon a meeting, and two days before the date the sultan sent gifts from shore: ten bulls, twenty sheep, and four dozen fowl arrived for distribution to the U.S. Navy ships. Moroccan troops and horses were paraded on the shore in an impressive show. The sultan himself made his way to the end of the stone breakwater to view the American ships through a telescope mounted on a tripod. Already he was much more deferential than Barbary leaders had been earlier in the face of smaller displays of power.

When the day of the meeting came—October 10—the American ships had for almost a week been kept in readiness for battle; as Preble noted in his diary, "All hands Slept at quarters." As agreed, Preble himself would go ashore, but he would not arrive in the company of a large delegation. Instead, his party would consist

Commander Preble's ships in the harbor at Tripoli.

only of himself, Consul Tobias Lear, and two midshipmen serving as aides.

At eleven o'clock, the four men prepared to go ashore, but before they did, Preble issued clear instructions. "If the least injury is offered to my person," he ordered those who remained aboard the ships, "immediately attack the batteries, the castle, the city and the troops, regardless of my personal safety."

Stephen Decatur and his men onboard the USS Philadelphia.

At one o'clock, the American delegation was summoned to the castle. The walk through the town did not impress Lear, and he noted the "very narrow and dirty streets [and] the wretched appearance of the inhabitants. . . . There appear to be no shops, no trade—nothing to please the eye or amuse the fancy." Upon reaching the castle, the Americans were ushered through a double file of guards, but Preble found that the sultan sat not on a throne but on the stone steps in a castle courtyard. One of the midshipmen reported his disappointment at the sight. "I had connected with the idea of Emperor of Morocco, something grand," he wrote to his mother back in South Carolina, "but what was my disappointment at seeing a small man, wrapped up in a woolen heik or cloak."

Faced with Preble's overwhelming navy, the sultan seemed

almost apologetic. He regretted the hostilities, he said through an interpreter. His country was at peace with the United States, and he would honor the treaty his father had made in 1786. He promised to punish the man who had ordered the attacks on the American ships. He would see to it that the captains of the pirate vessels paid dearly, too.

Then the sultan listened as Preble "endeavored to impress on his mind the advantages of a free commercial intercourse . . . and that the revenues of the Emperor arising from that source, would be much greater than any thing they could expect if at war with us." It was an American argument, a case made for free trade. And the sultan, confronted with America's newfound strength, was paying attention.

The following day, the sultan produced a letter for Jefferson. "Know Ye that all the Treaties entered into between the two nations, remain as they were," the sultan wrote. Several more days were required to exchange and translate the documents that made the understanding official, but the pressure was off.

Commodore Edward Preble had achieved a significant victory without firing a single shot. Just as remarkable was the fact that tribute had been neither paid nor promised. Preble put it simply in a letter home to his beloved, Mary Deering, in Maine, once he had returned to Gibraltar: "An honorable peace is established." A clear show of force, backed up by a genuine threat, had resulted in harmony between the nations.

CHAPTER 23

The Fate of the USS Philadelphia

Cruising off Tripoli according to Preble's orders, Captain William Bainbridge met with no pirate ships for nearly the entire month of October. The few suspicious ships sighted remained out of reach, staying within the protection of the gun batteries that lined the city walls overlooking the harbor.

At nine o'clock on the morning of October 31, some fifteen miles east of Tripoli, a suspicious sail was sighted near the coast. The *Philadelphia* gave chase. As if to taunt the much larger warship, the unidentified vessel hoisted the Tripolitan colors; it was a Barbary ship trying to slip the blockade. Now the race was on.

The *Philadelphia* was soon at full sail. Though well offshore, Bainbridge aimed to cut off the smaller vessel before she reached port. Increasing speed, the *Philadelphia* gained on the corsair, and as eleven o'clock neared, Bainbridge judged the little ship might be within range. He ordered the firing of the cannon mounted at the front of the ship. Wary of the unfamiliar waters off Tripoli—other American captains had reported uncharted obstacles and unpredictable winds near shore—three sailors took repeated depth soundings. They reported a depth of a safe forty feet and more, roughly twice the draft of the *Philadelphia*.

The USS Philadelphia *entering Tripoli harbor.*

The American gunners kept a constant fire as they chased the ship. By eleven thirty, the city grew closer and the fortress walls could be plainly seen. Rather than put his ship at risk of coming within range of the shore guns, Bainbridge reluctantly ordered the helmsman to change course. To his frustration, he had to accept that he could not overtake the Tripolitan pirates, and the *Philadelphia* began a long, slow turn into the wind, away from the city. The chase was over, and the pirates would go unpunished.

Moments later, the USS *Philadelphia* lurched. The ship's great frame shuddered as her bow rose a full six feet out of the water. One moment she was coursing through the sea at the land equivalent of roughly ten miles per hour; the next, she was fixed, immobile, a man-made wooden island halted less than two miles from shore.

The *Philadelphia* had run aground.

The captain stood stunned on the bridge. The charts indicated no reefs, and the last sounding had measured a more-than-sufficient thirty-five feet. But there was no time to wonder. The men aboard the *Philadelphia* needed to act to save their ship, stranded so close to the enemy stronghold.

By midafternoon, Bainbridge and his officers recognized their situation was hopeless. Bainbridge ordered the gunpowder dampened and the ship's pumps clogged with shot. He sent carpenters below with their augers to drill holes in the bottom, to make the ship unsailable once she was in Tripolitan hands. Bainbridge tore his copies of the American signaling codes into shreds and ordered the sheets set afire and thrown overboard. Pistols, muskets, cutlasses, pikes, and other weapons were tossed into the sea. If he had to hand over his ship to the bashaw, Bainbridge was going to make sure it was as worthless a prize as possible.

The battle of Tripoli.

CHAPTER 24

Prisoners

Ordered into the gunboats, the captives—Bainbridge and his 306 men—were forced to row toward land, their captors "standing with drawn sabres over our heads." Some men were thrown from the overcrowded boats into the sea, left to swim for shore—or drown.

When they landed at the base of the bashaw's palace, the captives were marched through the streets to jeers from the elated Tripolitans.

They were taken to what had been the American consulate prior to Consul Cathcart's departure. There they slept on the floor on mats and blankets. At Bainbridge's request, the man Cathcart had left in charge of American affairs, Danish consul Nicholas Nissen, was summoned. He promised to do what he could to provide basic comforts and, the following day, returned with mattresses, blankets, and baskets of fruit. In the months to come, he would be the conduit for money and goods sent to the prisoners.

The officers had the run of the abandoned house and received

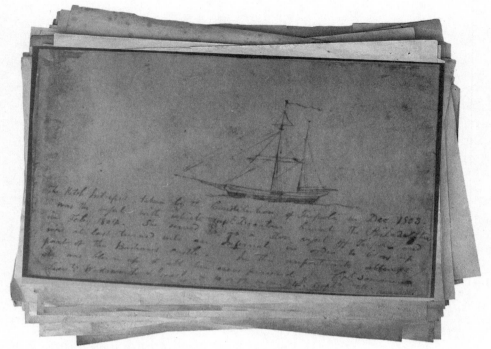

A sketch of the Intrepid *on which Decatur transported his men to the USS* Philadelphia.

adequate food, but the members of the crew faced real hardships. Many had arrived dripping wet and gratefully accepted the dry clothing other slaves brought in exchange for their waterlogged uniforms. That first night the crewmen were fed nothing and slept in an outdoor courtyard.

Bainbridge regarded the ship as beyond salvage, subject now to rot and ruin in the waves of the sea. The pirates sensed that a storm was brewing and hoped that with the wind rising, the morning would bring a storm surge that would lift the *Philadelphia* off the reef. The pirates had read the weather correctly. A violent gale powered by westerly winds raised the *Philadelphia*. The once-stranded ship, lifted off the reef by the rising tide, floated free, despite the holes drilled in her hull by her carpenters. Now in the full possession of the Tripolitans, with the possibility that it could be repaired and its guns refurbished, the *Philadelphia* had become a prize of which the bashaw could be well and truly proud. The second prong of Preble's strategy—the attack on Tripoli—had gone terribly wrong.

CHAPTER 25

A Spy Within the Walls

Preble had been busily gathering intelligence on the workings of Tripoli, and the best information came from William Bainbridge. From his prison in Tripoli, Bainbridge could see with his own eyes—and a spyglass provided by Consul Nissen—what happened in the harbor. He also had a means of communicating with the Americans; the bashaw permitted him to send letters, believing that a captive was his own best advocate for securing ransom payments. But because his captors read his letters before sending them, Bainbridge couldn't simply report on the results of his reconnaissance—at least not in the usual way.

Bainbridge found clandestine means by which to impart information that might be of military use. At first, he employed a cipher, coding his communications. When the bashaw started to suspect the code, Bainbridge resorted to "sympathetic ink," a diluted mix of lime or lemon juice. Using this method, invisible messages written between visible lines on a page emerged as a readable brown when held to a flame. Writing in letters and in books borrowed from the ever-helpful Consul Nissen, William Bainbridge helped Preble lay the groundwork for a secret scheme.

They would destroy the USS *Philadelphia* once and for all.

The orders made the operation sound simple. "Enter the Harbor in the night," Preble instructed. "Board the Frigate Philadelphia, burn her and make your retreat good." The recipient of those orders was Lieutenant Stephen Decatur Jr., with his two-ship fleet, the USS *Intrepid* and USS *Syren*.

Stephen Decatur

The plan called for the *Intrepid* to run ahead, as it had been rerigged with short masts and triangular sails, mimicking the look of local ships; its appearance should raise no alarms. The USS *Syren* would trail five miles behind. Decatur ordered most of his crew to remain below. Just six men at a time could walk the deck, and those who did wore the uniform of Maltese merchant sailors, with showy gold braid.

As darkness fell, the light of a crescent moon revealed the *Philadelphia* in silhouette. She was a heartrending sight to Decatur and his men. Her foremast remained a stump, and her upper yards were laid out on the deck. Stripped of sails, she could go nowhere under her own power. Yet her sheer scale seemed awesome in a harbor where little local boats skimmed the waves. To see the frigate's guns remounted and to imagine them manned by Tripoli pirates? That was too horrible even to contemplate.

As the *Intrepid* neared, a sharp-eyed Tripolitan on the *Philadelphia* spotted something amiss. Perhaps the anchors aboard the *Intrepid* had been seen. Maybe it was the glint of a sword worn by one of the dozens of sailors lying in the shadows cast by the bulwarks. Whatever the clue, the game was nearly up.

"Americanos!" came the cry.

Salvador Catalano answered. A Sicilian hired by Preble for his knowledge of Barbary harbors, Catalano was fluent in the common tongue of sailors in the southern Mediterranean, a mix of Berber, Arabic, Italian, Spanish, Portuguese, and Maltese. His manner unruffled, he offered assurances that only Maltese and Englishmen were aboard. With the message acknowledged, the men aboard the *Intrepid* continued to haul the hawsers, and the *Intrepid* had soon pulled up alongside the *Philadelphia*.

As the ships touched, Stephen Decatur issued a simple order, uttered as he himself leaped for the main chains of the *Philadelphia* to climb the dozen feet to the deck of the taller ship.

The one-word order—"Board!"—initiated a blur of action.

No gunshots echoed. Decatur had decreed that only blades were to be used, because the invaders wanted to attract as little attention as possible to the fight for the *Philadelphia*, which was moored just a few hundred yards from the fortress guns. Of the thirty or so Tripolitans aboard the ship, roughly a dozen ran for a boat and rowed for safety.

In less than ten minutes, the savage fight was over without having attracted the notice of sentries onshore, and the carefully planned torching of the ship could begin. A team of ten men went below to set fire to the berth deck and forward storeroom. A dozen men went deeper into the ship to the wardroom and steerage, and a third squad to the cockpit and a second storeroom. A fourth team manned the *Intrepid*'s cutter, patrolling the harbor.

The fire crews carried three-inch-long candles, with wicks

Decatur and the Dey of Algiers. 1815 [1815]

Decatur and the dey of Algiers.

Decatur and his men fighting hand-to-hand.

that had been immersed in turpentine to enhance their flammability, and each team had a pair of lanterns. With the Tripolitan defenders subdued, combustibles were swiftly handed up from the *Intrepid* and taken below. The disciplined operation proceeded with speed, and in a matter of minutes, the men waited at their stations for Decatur's next command.

Walking the deck from forward to aft, he called his simple order down each hatchway—"Fire!"—and the men, with their candles lit from the lanterns, ignited dozens of fires in every part of the ship.

As the men raced to return to the deck, columns of suffocating smoke rose from the hatches. Flames soon followed, as sailors and officers alike leaped back aboard the *Intrepid*. Decatur watched as the last of his men climbed down to the deck of the ketch; only one sailor had been wounded, none killed. Decatur himself would be the last man to step off the deck of the *Philadelphia*—and he did so in dramatic style, leaping into the rigging of the *Intrepid*.

The night of February 16, 1804, would be one that the imprisoned crew of the *Philadelphia* would never forget. The once-proud ship now lay on the rocks, free of her anchors after her cables burned. She was a smoking hulk, reduced to a long row of ribs barely visible at the waterline. The frigate would never be put to sea as a pirate ship.

The USS Philadelphia *in flames.*

Part

Three

CHAPTER 26

The Hamet Option

As plans were laid for the destruction of the USS *Philadelphia*, Preble was also developing a larger secret strategy. With Jefferson's and Madison's authorization, U.S. diplomats had continued talking to Hamet Qaramanli, brother of Yusuf. He still wanted his rightful

The burning of the USS Philadelphia *February 16, 1804.*

place on the throne as bashaw of Tripoli, but to get it he needed American help. When letters from Hamet's agents reached Preble, he arranged to meet the men in Malta.

Hamet had traveled to Alexandria, Egypt, they told Preble, and was still in exile. But he had a plan, too, and he also had followers. Hamet would assemble a large army of Arabs. If the Americans could help underwrite the venture and provide some naval support, this force might march overland from Egypt to Derne, a provincial capital in eastern Tripoli. With the help of American firepower from the sea, Hamet and Eaton believed Tripoli could be taken back.

Hamet also had a promise for the Americans, one that Preble knew would please his superiors. If the Americans aided him with money and military equipment in his quest, Hamet, once restored to his rightful place as bashaw, would release all slaves and captives, including the men who had been aboard the *Philadelphia*. He would also agree to a permanent peace with the United States. Furthermore, he would allow the U.S. Navy to make Tripoli its permanent base and station soldiers in the main fort.

Meanwhile, at home, the news of the *Philadelphia* had been good for William Eaton's pet cause. After his expulsion by the bey of Tunis in early March 1803, Eaton had returned to the United States. More than anything, Eaton wanted to persuade the powers that be to support his plan to replace Bashaw Yusuf on Tripoli's throne with the exiled Hamet Qaramanli. He also wanted to lead the expedition that would land in Alexandria, join Hamet, and march to Derne, as Preble schemed. Eaton was the driving force on the American

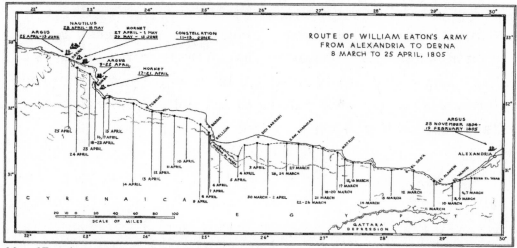

Map of Eaton's seven-week walk from Alexandria to Derne.

side, writing to the speaker of the House of Representatives and meeting with Secretary of State Madison and the other members of Jefferson's cabinet to detail his case. The secretary of war was skeptical, but the secretary of the navy, Robert Smith, was won over.

Eaton was ordered to act as a liaison with Hamet. Madison wrote to the Barbary chief consul, Tobias Lear, authorizing the plan, though he did so in his usual cautious fashion. "Of the co-operation of the Elder brother of the Bashaw of Tripoli we are . . . willing to avail ourselves." Madison also instructed Lear to make available to Eaton $20,000 to carry out the plan.

William Eaton, now a U.S. Navy agent for the Barbary regencies, traveled back to the Mediterranean on the ship carrying the man who would replace Commodore Preble, Commodore Samuel

Barron. Eaton used the crossing to fully brief the commodore and elicit his support. Barron was arriving on the Barbary Coast to face one hostile nation, Tripoli. Morocco, Tunis, and Algiers had drawn versions of peace treaties with the United States. But the bashaw of Tripoli was holding strong.

CHAPTER 27

Opening a New Front

Jefferson's government left the decision of whether to help Hamet in the hands of their men in the Mediterranean. The chief diplomat and the commodore, Lear and Barron, would have to approve Eaton's efforts if his plan was to move forward. Eaton's lawyerly arguments were strong. He maintained that only a ground campaign would force Yusuf into accepting a peace on American terms. He pointed out that the Americans most familiar with the politics of the region, Richard O'Brien and James Cathcart, had endorsed the idea of restoring Hamet as bashaw. And recently, they found that Captain Preble had, too.

But not all the American officials stationed in the Mediterranean and involved in Barbary affairs thought the mission a good one. Chief Consul Tobias Lear, the region's most important representative of the Department of State, complained that Hamet lacked the force or influence needed to make him helpful to the Americans.

Despite Lear's doubts, Eaton's plan received approval. He was authorized to find Hamet, negotiate with him, and raise an Arab army to help restore the rightful bashaw to power. These orders in hand, in November 1804 Eaton sailed for Egypt aboard the USS *Argus*. Built to hold 142 men, the snug ship easily took aboard Eaton's tiny army, which, at that moment, consisted solely of Eaton, two U.S. Navy midshipmen, and eight U.S. Marines.

Presley O'Bannon

If Eaton's band fell far short of the army he aimed to build, he still maintained high hopes—and one reason was the presence of the Marines and their leader, Lieutenant Presley O'Bannon. Eaton needed such men, skilled fighters on land and sea. Eaton's ten men amounted to a small start, of course, but these committed young fighters, Eaton believed, would soon be supplemented by Hamet's larger army in Egypt. They could also hire mercenaries to reinforce Hamet's loyal followers; thanks to his years in North Africa, Eaton understood the value of local soldiers, men acclimated to the unique demands of desert living. He also felt confident that disaffected Tripolitans would flock to Hamet's side once he marched back into his country. A fine team was in the making.

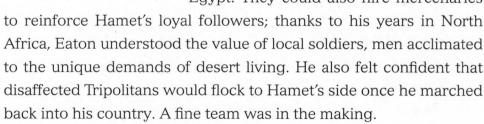

CHAPTER 28

Finding Hamet

Before Eaton and his Marines could help Hamet, though, they had to find him—and in 1804 no one seemed to know where Hamet Qaramanli was hiding. When the rumor had circulated, in July 1803, that Bashaw Yusuf had dispatched assassins to kill him in the eastern Tripolitan city of Derne, Hamet had run for his life, fleeing to Egypt. Reports indicated that the thin, soft-spoken former bashaw remained there. But where, exactly? Forced to be on the move out of fear of his brother's agents, he seemed to have disappeared into the sands of the Sahara.

Eaton's first port of call in November 1804 was the ancient city of Alexandria, Egypt. Eaton recognized that he needed Egyptian help if he was to find Hamet. Accordingly, he befriended local people, and over candies and coffee, he learned that the man he sought was upriver. He was told that Hamet had joined forces with the Mamelukes, the sworn enemies of the Ottoman Empire and, more immediately, the powers that controlled the mouth of the river. Supposing he found Hamet, how was Eaton to extract him and his supporters when they would have to travel through Ottoman territory? Despite these challenges, William Eaton, having persuaded a president, a government, and the U.S. Navy to support his scheme, gamely headed up the Nile to Cairo. There he would next make his case to the viceroy of Egypt.

Letters from the British consul gained Eaton an audience with the Egyptian viceroy in Cairo. He told the viceroy that he was seeking Hamet, and explained that America had no interest in occupying Tripoli. The United States sought only to defend its own citizens and interests from unwarranted attack. Several nervous weeks passed before the messengers located the former bashaw, and they delivered Eaton's message to him on January 3. Five days later, Eaton received Hamet's eager reply.

The former bashaw was ready for the expedition, confident "that God will aid us in establishing peace and tranquility." On February 5, 1805, Eaton and Hamet, who had met years earlier in Tunis, were reunited outside Cairo.

Taking it upon himself to represent the United States of America, Eaton negotiated with the former bashaw concerning their respective promises. Hamet needed to be sure the Americans would support him. Eaton needed assurances that Hamet would treat Americans well once he was in power. Their conversations yielded a formal agreement.

With the treaty in place, the plan that William Eaton had been shaping for more than three years was about to unfold. America, pounding Tripoli from the sea, would soon be continuing the attack on land. Together, Eaton and Hamet would raise a mercenary army that would join the Marines for a historic march across more than five hundred miles of rocky desert to Derne, Tripoli's second-largest city. Once Derne had fallen, they would march west to Benghazi. They would capture that city, and then U.S. warships would carry them the last four hundred miles to take Tripoli. It was a bold plan, but despite the doubts of Lear and others, Eaton was confident that it could work.

CHAPTER 29

The March

On March 6, 1805, the trek began. Four hundred men set out from Alexandria, Egypt. Their goal: to change the history of the Barbary Coast. Among their number were just ten Americans: William Eaton, Lieutenant O'Bannon, a midshipman, a Marine sergeant, and six Marine privates. Hamet brought along ninety Tripolitans. The rest were hired mercenaries, mostly Greek and Arab cavalrymen and foot soldiers. It was a long caravan, led from the front with martial efficiency but diminishing to pack animals with supplies well to the rear.

Newly self-declared "General, and Commander in Chief of the land forces," William Eaton marched proudly in uniform, epaulets on his shoulders, his hat decorated with lace, his buttons and spurs polished brass. One of the oddest—and yet most effective—military campaigns in American history had begun, with General Eaton leading the charge.

The march to Derne had barely started before a mutiny jeopardized the whole trip. After just three days of marching along the coast, the camel handlers hired to guide the pack animals demanded to be paid in advance. When an irresolute Hamet did nothing, Eaton threatened to abandon the expedition. The handlers quieted, not wanting to risk losing the pay they were promised, and the little revolutionary army marched on, averaging roughly twenty miles a day. The long column soon encountered incessant rain

On the way to Derne.

blowing in from the coast, which soaked the men and their supplies. Temperatures rose to almost 100 degrees Fahrenheit by day and plunged to near freezing at night. The Sahara was not making Eaton's task easy.

After almost a month of marching, Eaton's army encountered a large camp of several thousand Bedouins, nomadic people who traveled the North African continent. "We were the first Christians ever seen by these wild people," Eaton observed. Just as he had hoped, the ranks of his little army began to swell. Eighty mounted warriors joined from the Bedouins, and by early April, Eaton counted "between six and seven hundred fighting men on the

Eaton's forces used camels to transport goods.

ground, exclusive of followers of the camp and Bedouin families, who inclusively make a body of about twelve hundred people." As it marched across the plateau that overlooked the seas, Eaton's army was becoming more formidable, ready to take on the official Tripolitan forces.

But there was trouble ahead. Rations became scarce. Water supplies dwindled. Eventually the Arabs in the force refused to go on until they had assurances that U.S. supply ships awaited them at Bomba, about ninety miles away. Scouts were sent ahead to check the harbor. At first, there were no ships in sight. But the next morning, the first of two arrived. "Language is too poor to paint the joy and exultation which this messenger of life excited in every breast," Eaton wrote.

After reaching Bomba, the army feasted and refreshed itself until, on April 23, the marchers resumed their progress toward Derne. En route again, word reached the caravan that Bashaw Yusuf had heard about their march and had dispatched an army to defend Derne. The news dampened the recently buoyant spirits of Eaton's army and made Hamet fear for himself and his family.

CHAPTER 30

At the City Gates

On April 25, 1805, the army made camp on a ridge overlooking Derne.

The next morning, Eaton sent a letter to the governor of Derne. "I want no territory," his message read. "With me is advancing the legitimate Sovereign of your country—give us a passage through your city, and for the supplies of which we shall have need, you will receive fair compensation. . . . I shall see you tomorrow in a way of your choice."

By early afternoon, Eaton had his reply. "The flag of truce was sent back to me," he wrote, "with this laconic answer, 'My head or yours!'"

As the sun rose over the Sahara on April 27, Hamet, William Eaton, Presley O'Bannon, and their unlikely army of mercenaries, midshipmen, Marines, Greeks, Arabs, and Bedouins—a brave band of misfits—prepared to storm the city gates.

Eaton's plan called for an attack on Derne on three fronts. First, from the sea, the guns aboard the three American ships would bombard the city. Second, using field guns sent by Barron, Eaton and his men would fire upon the walls of the city from the southeast. Finally, a wave of men led by Hamet Qaramanli would descend on the rear of the town from the west.

That morning, the *Nautilus* brought Eaton's guns to shore. There, a narrow beach immediately gave way to a steep climb, and the task of hauling a heavy carronade up the slope with block and tackle proved time-consuming. Eager to get to the coming fight, Eaton decided to settle for just one artillery piece.

Finally, at one thirty in the afternoon, the assault began. From a distance of half a mile out to sea, the *Argus* and the *Nautilus* began firing into the town. From their vantage on the hillside, O'Bannon and his men maintained a steady musket fire, accompanied by round shot from the carronade. With the *Hornet* positioned in the bay to

General Eaton and Hamet Qaramanli lead their troops to Derne.

fire on the city from a distance of just one hundred yards, Derne was taking heavy bombardment.

At first, the attack seemed to go well. Within forty-five minutes, Derne's harbor guns fell silent. Under heavy fire from the U.S. Navy ships, the Tripolitans operating the harbor guns had withdrawn and moved to reinforce the defenders of the more vulnerable south wall.

Eaton's cannoneers kept up their fire until a cannonball shattered their rammer, the long wooden tool used to drive the shot and powder wad down the bore of the large gun. No longer able to load and fire the gun, the men around O'Bannon and Eaton were thrown into confusion.

Thinking fast, Eaton saw but one alternative: he ordered a charge down the hill, directly into the teeth of the enemy's defense. The odds were not in his favor, but he remained undaunted.

"We rushed forward against a host of savages more than ten to our one." On horseback, Eaton led the charge at a gallop, an intimidating sight as he swung his custom-made scimitar over his head. By some miracle, he was not injured by the enemy's gunfire, though he would find five bullet holes in his robes.

On the other side of town, Hamet and his troops occupied an old castle. Eaton had instructed the Tripolitan to lead his force of more than seven hundred men—some on foot, others on horseback—and attack the city via a deep ravine southwest of Derne. Sheiks sympathetic to the former bashaw had advised that he could expect support from most of the population in that part of the city. Other horsemen in Hamet's force were to take positions in the surrounding hills to the rear, ready to cut off any Tripolitan forces attempting to retreat from the city.

As a dense cloud of blue smoke rose from the harbor, Eaton was delighted to see Hamet's horsemen swooping down to the city. Knowing that Hamet's army was fighting fiercely on the other side of the city emboldened him for a daring charge of the city walls. Cannon fire from the ships offered cover as Eaton, O'Bannon, and their men crossed the beach, but the men still faced volleys of musket balls from the ramparts.

One of O'Bannon's seven Marines fell, seriously wounded. Another took a bullet to the chest, dying immediately. Then Eaton himself took a musket ball to the left wrist. Yet the wave of men and their flashing bayonets continued their charge.

To the surprise of the small brigade of invaders, the city's defenders began to retreat into the city as the Americans approached. The frontal assault produced a growing panic. The ragged fire from behind the walls ceased, and the Tripolitan defenders melted into the dizzying maze of the city's twisting streets and stacked houses. The bashaw's army managed only sporadic fire as they retreated.

With Eaton wounded, O'Bannon took full command. Breaching the city's walls, he led the charge directly to the oceanfront guns. There, after lowering the bashaw's ensign, O'Bannon planted the American flag on the ramparts. He then turned the enemy's own guns on them; abandoned in a rush during the naval bombardment, many were still loaded, powdered, and ready to fire. In a matter of minutes, the Americans held the high ground and the artillery.

Meanwhile, at the other end of town, Hamet's flag could now be

Capture of Derne.

seen flying from the governor's palace. After years of planning, months of preparations, and a fifty-two-day march that covered more than five hundred miles, the city had fallen in the short span of two and a half hours.

All told, there were fourteen dead and wounded among the contingent of Americans and Greeks led by Eaton and O'Bannon. Two of the dead were O'Bannon's Marines. The number of casualties among Hamet's party and the Tripolitan forces was not recorded but totaled in the hundreds.

Eaton was elated. His plan had worked thus far, and an army of fewer than a thousand men had overrun a fighting force of four thousand. The governor of Derne was still at large—he found refuge in a mosque—but Eaton felt certain that the victory would win many Tripolitans to Hamet's side, and that it would demonstrate to the world that the Americans were not to be trifled with. Eaton had proved that distance was no barrier to the Americans and had put the world on notice that Hamet, the rightful ruler of Tripoli, had his sights set on regaining his throne and his family. Rejoicing at the prospect of victory, Hamet is said to have offered his sword to O'Bannon as a token of his thanks.

Word of the fall of Derne was bound to anger and panic the bashaw. Hamet and the Americans were coming for him, and Bashaw Yusuf knew it.

CHAPTER 31

The Other Front

With Eaton's resounding victory in Derne, a military victory in Tripoli seemed within reach. But Tobias Lear had other plans. He wanted a diplomatic deal, and a deal is what he made.

A few weeks before the attack on Derne, Bashaw Yusuf had shown signs of wanting to make peace—but only on his terms. In return for $200,000, he promised to release Captain Bainbridge and the men of the USS *Philadelphia*. Though desperate for a deal, Lear recognized the offer for the extortion it was and rejected it. Then the news of the capture of Derne arrived, and Lear saw his great chance. He felt certain that the news of Hamet's victory would strike fear into Bashaw Yusuf—and he was right.

Lear underestimated the effect of Eaton's victory on the Barbary powers. Aboard the USS *Constitution*, Lear took what he thought was a hard position: he offered $60,000 in payment for the freedom of the *Philadelphia*'s captives and refused to go ashore until the bashaw agreed to his terms.

The relieved bashaw saw a chance to save his throne. He accepted the deal, and by June 3, the terms were agreed upon. Two days later, Colonel Lear went into the city and was welcomed into the palace. Peace was declared and the prisoners freed—but the achievement was tainted. Lear had paid for the release of American prisoners, and even worse, he had betrayed Eaton and Hamet. As part of the deal, Lear had promised that all American forces would evacuate Derne.

CHAPTER 32

Stunned

Unaware of Lear's negotiations, Eaton, Hamet, and their men stood firm as their enemies counterattacked. Eaton feared that either his supplies or the nerves of his men would give out. The brave liberators of Derne held the city securely, but they could not hold out indefinitely without supplies and reinforcements.

Yet Eaton could do little but wait for the American response to his call for support. When the response came, it did not come in the form of the men, munitions, and other aid he had requested. Instead, he got a letter advising him that the peace process had begun and no further advancement of his army would be necessary or supported.

Eaton was stunned.

Even more stunning was the accompanying order for him to abandon Derne and come home. The flabbergasted Eaton, who had fully expected to carry his fight to Benghazi and even Tripoli, was told to give up the ground purchased with his men's blood and to renege on his promises to Hamet.

Eaton remained in place. He refused to accept that he would be forced to return hard-won ground to the pirates. Then, on June 11, another ship sailed into Derne harbor bringing a new message.

This time, it was the USS *Constellation*, and the dispatches that came ashore included one from Tobias Lear, dated five days earlier. Lear wrote that the bravery of the Americans had impressed the bashaw and that the result had been a formal end to the war. Word of Lear's treaty was a blow to Eaton from which he would never recover.

Even as the victor at Derne accepted that he had little choice but to leave, Eaton realized that withdrawal would be a delicate matter. If word leaked that the American forces were preparing to depart, enemy forces might be emboldened to attack. That meant the Americans must leave in secrecy.

Behaving as if nothing had changed, Eaton spent the next day inspecting the garrison and issuing orders as usual. Then, at eight o'clock in the evening, he posted the Marines in a conspicuous place, hoping they would serve as a decoy. Over the next several hours, the rest of the small American force was ferried to the *Constellation* as unobtrusively as possible. Eaton then summoned the outraged and brokenhearted Hamet, who reluctantly joined the retreat because he had no choice but to accept that pursuing the battle without American help was impossible. The Marines, the officers, and Eaton went last. There could be no farewells, no ceremony. Just a quiet exit, a retreat that felt shameful.

When Hamet's Arab allies discovered that the Americans had left, they panicked. Once the bashaw's men learned the news, they would take out their fury on those left behind. Humiliated and betrayed, the sympathetic Arabs ran for the mountains, abandoning the town. In Tripoli there might be peace, but the citizens of Derne who had embraced Hamet would pay a heavy price for their support.

A Senate committee would later investigate what had unfolded in Tripoli that June. Eaton's old friend Senator Timothy Pickering would offer a blistering condemnation of Lear, describing his conduct as "nothing but the basest treachery on the basest principles." The committee strongly criticized the treaty as an "inglorious deed." Yet the Senate still mustered the required two-thirds majority to ratify the Treaty of Peace and Amity between the United States and Tripoli. Whatever the disagreements about the way in which it had come to pass, the peace, at that moment, became an established fact.

CHAPTER 33

An Incomplete Victory

The new Barbary peace truly was a victory, though an incomplete one. For President Jefferson, who received the news of Lear's treaty on September 6, 1805, the end of the conflict with Tripoli was a great relief. The war that had dogged his administration for more than four years was finally at an end—and it had ended Jefferson's way.

The *National Intelligencer* proclaimed victory: "Our captive countrymen have been restored to the bosom of their country. . . . We have got what we wanted." American shipping could flow freely again. The most essential goal in declaring war had been accomplished.

The country cheered the heroes as they returned to the United States. In mid-September, William Bainbridge arrived, already cleared of blame for the loss of the USS *Philadelphia*. He stepped off the ship along with 117 of his officers and crewmen, and they were feted with awards, honors, and a warm welcome. Other returning captains and captives were paraded down main streets and toasted as heroes, too.

A complete victory over the Barbary pirates would come under another president, but for now America had much to be grateful for. The murky ending of the Barbary War didn't take away from the fact that America had stood up to the pirates, something that most of the more established European nations hadn't been willing to do. America had held firm and fought, and now the young nation's navy had the experience it would need to take on Britain in the War of 1812. Like the Barbary War, that war would begin with devastating losses but end with a huge leap in respect from the world.

CHAPTER 34

The Legacy

When it unfolded, the first Barbary War was no more than a ripple in the much larger waters of world politics. Bashaw Yusuf had declared war on America with the absurd act of chopping down an American flagstaff. Thomas Jefferson, as president of the first democracy of the modern era, responded in a manner that he, as one of the great political philosophers of his or any time, thought right. Today, the war's military legacy cannot be ignored. It saw the emergence of the U.S. Navy as a force to be reckoned with in foreign seas. It saw the American flag planted for the first time in victory on terrain outside the western hemisphere. It saw the first fight in which U.S. Navy gunfire worked in concert with U.S. land forces. So great was the war's significance for the Marines that their hymn refers to "the shores of Tripoli," and the Marine Corps adopted the Mameluke sword as part of its officers' uniforms in 1825.

Decatur receiving the dey of Algiers.

To Jefferson's way of thinking, the captivity of American seamen and the interference with American commerce demanded a strong military response. He had been considering this for many years. It had been the subject of many discussions between him and his friend John Adams, back in their ministerial days, in 1780s Europe. In fact, they had set the terms of the debate very clearly.

Adams had told his solemn friend he thought it possible to buy a peace.

Jefferson had countered, "I should prefer the obtaining of it by war."

In response to events on the Barbary Coast, Jefferson, in 1801, had dispatched a small U.S. Navy squadron to the Mediterranean. For the next four years, he responded to circumstances, expanding the fleet to a much larger naval presence. In the end, thanks to the bold leadership of men like Preble and Decatur and Eaton and O'Bannon, military force had helped regain national honor. Even the Federalists, who liked little that Jefferson did, came to accept that the United States needed to play a military role in overseas affairs.

Many men and women suffered in captivity before America's intervention rid the world of North African piracy, but their suffering was not in vain. After centuries of conflict along the Barbary Coast, only the exercise of military strength had succeeded. The lesson was not lost on America. The young nation gained from this chapter the courage to exercise its strength in the world, and it would remember that lesson in the future when other innocent lives were at stake.

A print showing "Naval Heroes of the United States." Decatur at top center, Preble middle right, Dale center bottom, and Bainbridge middle left.

APPENDIXES

The Barbary Coast

From about 700 BCE to 1830 CE, piracy was common practice on the southern Mediterranean Sea and along the coasts of Spain and Portugal. The area became known as the Barbary Coast. The term "Barbary" refers to the Berber people, one of the original peoples who settled there. The Berber people lived in the lands spanning the Mediterranean Sea and the Sahara Desert from at least 2000 BCE. Some were nomadic, herding sheep and goats across mountains and deserts. Others set up trade routes across thousands of miles. The Berber culture remains vibrant today in the North African countries of Morocco, Algeria, Tunisia, Libya, Egypt, Mali, Niger, and Mauritania.

In Jefferson's time, the countries along the coast were Morocco to the far west, followed by Algiers, Tunis, and Tripoli. Today, the countries are known as Morocco, Algeria, Tunisia, and Libya, respectively. The people were Muslim, practicing the religion of Islam. The Quran is the Islamic holy book.

The nations did not bring in enough cash by raising animals, selling crops, and trading. So the rulers authorized pirates to capture foreign merchant ships in exchange for a portion of the profits. The profits came from the sale of the cargo the ships carried as well as the sale of the crew into slavery.

Frigates and Galleys

The Naval Act of 1794 provided for the construction of six warships, called frigates. In order to get them built quickly, President Washington chose six ports along the Atlantic to do the work:

Portsmouth, New Hampshire: the USS *Congress*
Boston, Massachusetts: the USS *Constitution*
New York, New York: the USS *President*
Philadelphia, Pennsylvania: the USS *United States*
Baltimore, Maryland: the USS *Constellation*
Gosport, Virginia: the USS *Chesapeake*

The work of building these frigates carried a total cost of $688,888.82, a huge sum of money for the new country.

These ships had three masts and were heavily armed with long guns and cannons. They were made of oak, a tree that was abundant in the country. The hull could be as much as twenty-five inches thick, making the ship strong and hard to damage. (That is the reason the USS *Constitution* was given the nickname "Old Ironsides.")

Innovations in shipbuilding in the new country resulted in frigates that could outrun much heavier ships—or keep pace with them in heavy seas.

Pirate ships, by contrast, used their space for men, not cannons. Each ship carried hundreds of sailors to board target ships and fight,

Top: A typical galley used by countries of North Africa.

Bottom: Many slaves powered the Barbary galleys.

and whole crews to sail captured ships home. One common type of pirate ship was the galley, a long ship that used its sails as secondary power and its oarsmen, who were slaves, as primary power. Up to six men pulled each oar. The rowers would maneuver the pirate ship next to a target ship so the pirates could board.

The galley was also thin and fast, with one cannon in front. The ship's pointed front was used to ram enemy vessels. A galley was not suited to the open ocean but was very effective on the calm waters of the Mediterranean Sea.

There was one schooner in Jefferson's first flotilla, the *Enterprise*. It had two masts and was very fast in open water but not as agile along the coast. Once the schooner arrived in Algiers, it was used to obtain and ferry supplies to the larger frigates.

Weapons

For close-range combat, pirates used flintlock pistols with skull-crushing butt caps at the end of the stock, and swords called scimitars, with a curved blade and often an intricately decorated handle.

U.S. Navy sailors and Marines carried personal pistols and had muskets at their disposal, but relied on huge cannons made of iron, running as long as nine feet and weighing as much as five thousand pounds. Each cannon was fitted into a carriage with wheels that was then tied to the ship. This prevented the cannon from sliding across the deck when it recoiled after being shot. It took around fifteen men to operate a cannon, loading the powder, packing it, lighting it, and cleaning it.

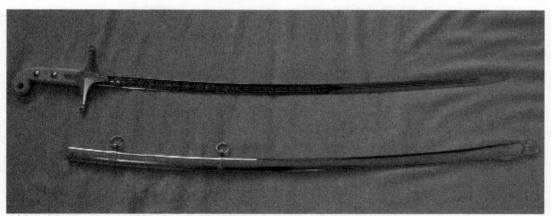

A Mameluke sword and scabbard, part of the Marine Corps dress uniform.

U.S. Marine Corps

John Adams, the second president of the United States, reactivated the U.S. Marines when he created the U.S. Navy in 1798. The Marines, before then known as the Continental Marines, were founded in 1775, and executed their first raid in 1776. The British, at war with their American colonies, were storing supplies for the war in the Bahamas. The Marines and the U.S. Navy successfully raided the supplies, sailing away with a large stash of gunpowder and cannons.

The monument to the heroes of the battle of Tripoli now at the United States Naval Academy in Annapolis, Maryland. It is the oldest military monument in the country.

During the Barbary Wars, Marines were invaluable during boarding actions and landing expeditions, and they also served to protect a ship's officers in the event of a mutiny by the crew.

After the Battle of Derne, Lieutenant Presley O'Bannon was presented with a curved sword modeled after the Mameluke scimitar. The victory is immortalized in the "Marines' Hymn." Here is the first verse:

> *From the Halls of Montezuma*
> *To the shores of Tripoli;*
> *We fight our country's battles*
> *In the air, on land, and sea;*
> *First to fight for right and freedom*
> *And to keep our honor clean;*
> *We are proud to claim the title*
> *Of United States Marine.*

Montezuma refers to the 1847 Battle of Chapultepec during the Mexican-American War.

U.S. Navy

On October 13, 1775, the Continental Congress, then the governing body of the thirteen colonies, voted to arm two ships for war. The British were superior at sea, in number of ships, experience, and firepower, and British ships had been blockading colonial ports, which meant that supplies couldn't get in and that trade between the colonies and Europe was at a standstill.

By the end of the Revolutionary War, more than fifty ships had been outfitted to defend the colonies. After the war, the ships were sold and their officers and crew returned to their homes.

Close-up of cannon aboard the refurbished USS Constitution, *the oldest ship in the U.S. Navy that remains afloat.*

The Constitution of the United States, ratified in 1789, authorized the creation of a navy. In response to the attacks by Barbary pirates, the navy's first six frigates were built and launched. In 1798, President Adams reassigned control of the navy from the Department of War to the newly created Department of the Navy.

Bainbridge Codes

Invisible ink was widely used in Europe and the colonies in the 1700s. George Washington used the technique to communicate with his spies at the beginning of the Revolutionary War.

You can communicate using invisible ink, too. You can write a message on a piece of paper that will seem blank, or write your message between the lines of visible sentences written in pencil or pen.

Lemon juice, onion juice, and milk make good ink. (Milk and lemon juice are easy to use. Onion juice is smelly and harder to make.)

For lemon juice, cut a lemon in half and squeeze the juice out into a bowl. For milk ink, simply pour milk into a bowl. Making onion ink requires a three-step process: Cut the onion in half. Grate some of it carefully into a bowl. Let it stand until you see liquid gathering in the bottom of the bowl. This liquid is the ink.

Use the heaviest white paper you can find.

Your writing instrument can be the end of a chopstick, a toothpick, or a cotton swab.

Now, let's see if you can expose what you've written.

For lemon juice and onion juice messages, pass the paper carefully over the top of a hot toaster. Be sure to wear oven mitts while doing this.

For milk messages, you'll need to rub graphite over the paper. The lead in pencils is graphite. You can get some from a pencil sharpener drawer, or you can ask an adult to scrape some off of a pencil. Rub the graphite gently over the paper and your message will appear.

There are many other ways to make up codes and send secret messages. These three books have lots of ideas:

Blackwood, Gary. *Mysterious Messages: A History of Codes and Ciphers*. New York: Scholastic, 2009.

Janeczko, Paul B. *Top Secret: A Handbook of Codes, Ciphers, and Secret Writing*. Cambridge, Mass.: Candlewick Press, 2004.

O'Brien, Eileen, and Diana Riddell. *The Usborne Book of Secret Codes*. London: Usborne Publishing, 1997.

Where to See Nineteenth-Century Ships Today

USS *Constitution*, Boston, Massachusetts
Frigate, launched October 21, 1797
Oldest commissioned navy vessel still afloat
www.nps.gov/bost/learn/historyculture/ussconst.htm

USS *Constellation*, Baltimore, Maryland
Sloop of war, launched August 26, 1854, using a small amount of material from the original *Constellation*
www.nps.gov/thingstodo/board-the-uss-constellation.htm

Visit Thomas Jefferson's Home, Monticello

Monticello was Thomas Jefferson's home, and he designed and supervised its construction. The plantation originally produced tobacco and then wheat as its cash crop. Slaves worked the land. The gardens of Monticello were Jefferson's laboratory. He experimented with growing vegetables not native to North America, including plants that were then considered only tropical, such as sweet potatoes, lima beans, and peanuts.

www.nps.gov/NR/travel/presidents/jefferson_monticello.html

"All my wishes end, where I hope my days will end—at Monticello."—THOMAS JEFFERSON.

Thomas Jefferson's beloved Monticello near Charlottesville, Virginia.

Timeline

1783

SEPTEMBER 3, 1783

The United States and Great Britain sign the Treaty of Paris, ending the Revolutionary War.

1784

SUMMER 1784

Thomas Jefferson sails to Europe to negotiate trade agreements.

1785

MAY 17, 1785

Jefferson becomes minister to France.

JULY 30, 1785

Algerian pirates capture the merchant ship *Dauphin*, Captain Richard O'Brien, and his crew.

1786

JUNE 28, 1786

The United States and Morocco sign a peace treaty.

1789

MARCH 4, 1789

The Constitution of the United States takes effect, providing for the creation of a navy.

APRIL 30, 1789
George Washington becomes the first president of the United States.

1790

MARCH 22, 1790
Jefferson becomes secretary of state.

1793

DECEMBER 1793
Jefferson resigns and returns to Monticello.

1794

MARCH 27, 1794
The Naval Act passes, authorizing the construction of the first six frigates in the U.S. Navy.

1797

MARCH 4, 1797
John Adams is inaugurated as the second president of the United States.

1797
The USS *United States* (May 10), the USS *Constellation* (September 7), and the USS *Constitution* (October 21) are launched.

1797
The crew of the *Dauphin* are released.

1801

MARCH 4, 1801
Thomas Jefferson is inaugurated as the third president of the United States.

MAY 11, 1801
Tripoli declares war on the United States.

JUNE 2, 1801
The first flotilla sets sail for the Strait of Gibraltar.

JULY 24, 1801
The USS *President* and the USS *Enterprise* reach Tripoli harbor.

AUGUST 1, 1801
The USS *Enterprise* engages in battle with the *Tripoli*.

1802

FEBRUARY 6, 1802
Congress approves Jefferson's request to use force against the Barbary nations.

1803

MARCH 1803
William Eaton is expelled from Tunis.

OCTOBER 31, 1803
William Bainbridge surrenders the USS *Philadelphia* to Tripoli.

1804

FEBRUARY 16, 1804

Stephen Decatur and his crew set the USS *Philadelphia* on fire.

1805

APRIL 27, 1805

William Eaton takes the fort at Derne, with support from the navy and mercenary troops.

JUNE 3, 1805

William Bainbridge and his remaining crew are released from captivity.

JUNE 4, 1805

The United States and Tripoli sign the Treaty of Peace and Amity, ending this era of war along the Barbary Coast.

Note: The Second Barbary War: While the United States was occupied fighting the British in the War of 1812, the dey of Algiers returned to piracy. In 1815, President James Madison formed a plan to stop the activity once and for all. From June 17–19, ten U.S. Navy ships under the command of Stephen Decatur captured two Algerian ships and took five hundred crew members prisoner. The two countries exchanged prisoners and signed a peace treaty that was ratified by the U.S. Senate on December 5, 1815.

Notes

Prologue

"Our sufferings are beyond our expression": Richard O'Brien to Thomas Jefferson, August 24, 1785.

Chapter 3

"hooping cough": Elizabeth Wayles Eppes to Thomas Jefferson, October 13, 1784.

"cannot live without you . . . talk French": Thomas Jefferson to Mary Jefferson, September 20, 1785.

"The vessel should have performed . . . a careful gentleman": Thomas Jefferson to Francis Eppes, August 30, 1785.

Chapter 4

"absolutely suspended between": Thomas Jefferson to Nathaniel Greene, January 12, 1785

"We are waiting with the greatest patience": M. Le Veillard to Benjamin Franklin, October 9, 1785.

Chapter 5

"If it is not done": John Adams to Thomas Jefferson, July 3, 1786.

"Buy a peace . . . constant cruise": Thomas Jefferson to John Adams, July 11, 1786.

"We ought not to fight them": John Adams to Thomas Jefferson, July 31, 1786.

Chapter 6

"If they refuse a [fair treaty]": Thomas Jefferson to James Monroe, November 11, 1784.

"It rests with Congress to decide": "Mediterranean Trade," December 30, 1790.

Chapter 7

"To cruise against": David Humphreys to Michael Murphy, October 6, 1793.

"I have not slept since Receipt": Edward Church to Thomas Jefferson, October 12, 1793.

Chapter 8

"take charge of the interests": "Appointment of Joel Barlow as U.S. Agent, Algiers," February 10, 1796.

Chapter 9

"periodical tribute or farther payment": Treaty of Peace and Friendship Between the United States of America and the Bey and Subjects of Tripoli of Barbary.

"Let your government": "Treaty of Peace and Friendship Between the United States of American and the Bey and Subjects of Tripoli of Barbary."

"See there our executive power Commissioned": William Eaton to Timothy Pickering, June 24, 1800.

"Shall the squadron now at Norfolk": Jefferson, notes, May 15, 1801–April 8, 1803.

Chapter 10

"I am convinced that the Bashaw": James L. Cathcart, "Circular Letter," February 21, 1801.

"The Bashaw has sent me": James L. Cathcart to James Madison, May 11, 1801.

"At a quarter past two": James L. Cathcart to James Madison, May 11, 1801.

Chapter 11

"Should you fall in with any": Richard Dale to Andrew Sterett, July 30, 1801.

Chapter 12

"the Profound respect" . . . "regalia due to him": Commerce": Richard Dale to the dey of Algiers and the bey of Tunis, July 10, 1801.

Chapter 13

"I am sorry to Inform": Richard Dale to the bashaw of Tripoli, July 25, 1801

"to take in as much water": Richard Dale to Andrew Sterett, July 30, 1801.

Chapter 14

"& Suffer'd him to proceed on": Newton Keene to William W. Burrows, August 10, 1801.

Chapter 15

"After a heavy slaughter": Thomas Jefferson, "Presidential Message," December 8, 1801.

Chapter 16

"kind of Enfluenza": Newton Keene to William W. Burrows, September 28, 1801.

Chapter 17

"to attack the usurper. . . . promote the scheme": William Eaton to James Madison, September 5, 1801.

Chapter 18

"I am convinced that Tripoli": Richard O'Brien to James Madison, July 22, 1801.

Chapter 19

"holding out the olive Branch": Secretary of the navy to Richard V. Morris, April 20, 1802.

"advanced period of the season": Richard V. Morris to the secretary of the navy, October 15, 1802.

Chapter 20

"You will upon receipt of this": Secretary of the navy to Richard V. Morris, June 21, 1803.

"captain Morris did not . . . want of capacity": "Concerning Commodore Morris' Squadron in the Mediterranean."

Chapter 21

"Your experience in affairs": Secretary of the navy to Edward Preble, August 2, 1803.

Chapter 22

"nothing will keep the [villains]": Edward Preble to the secretary of the navy, September 23, 1803.

"All hands Slept at quarters": Edward Preble, Diary, October 6, 1803.

"If the least injury is offered": Edward Preble, quoted in Tucker, Dawn Like Thunder, p. 205.

"very narrow and dirty streets": Tobias Lear to Mrs. Lear, October 13, 1803.

"I had connected with the idea": Ralph Izard Jr. to Mrs. Ralph Izard Sr., October 11, 1803.

"endeavored to impress on his mind": Edward Preble to the secretary of the navy, October 10, 1803.

"Know Ye that all the Treaties": Emperor of Morocco to Thomas Jefferson, October 11, 1803.

"An honorable peace is established": Edward Preble to Mary Deering, ca. October 1803.

Chapter 24

"standing with drawn sabres": Cowdery, in Baepler, *White Slaves, African Masters*, p. 162.

Chapter 25

"Enter the Harbor in the night": Edward Preble to Stephen Decatur, January 31, 1804.

Chapter 26

"Of the co-operation of the Elder": James Madison to Tobias Lear, June 6, 1804.

Chapter 28

"that God will aid us": Hamet Qaramanli to William Eaton, January 3, 1805.

Chapter 29

"We were the first Christians . . . twelve hundred people": William Eaton, "Journal," April 2, 1805; in Prentiss, *Life of the Late Gen. William Eaton*, p. 317.

"Language is too poor": William Eaton, "Journal," April 16, 1805; ibid., p. 329.

Chapter 30

"I want no territory . . . your choice": William Eaton to the governor of Derne, April 26, 1805; in Prentiss, *Life of the Late Gen. William Eaton*, p. 337.

"The flag of truce": William Eaton to Samuel Barron, April 29, 1805; ibid., p. 337.

"We rushed forward against a host": William Eaton to Samuel Barron, April 29, 1805; ibid., p. 337.

Chapter 32

"nothing but the basest treachery": Timothy Pickering to unknown, March 21, 1806.

"inglorious deed": "Report of the Committee," March 17, 1806.

Chapter 33

"Our captive countrymen": *National Intelligencer*, November 6, 1805.

"I should prefer the obtaining of it": Thomas Jefferson to John Adams, July 11, 1786.

For Further Information

Lincoln, Margarette. *The Pirate's Handbook*. New York: Dutton Books, 1995.

The author was the head of research at the National Maritime Museum in London, England, and helped prepare their acclaimed exhibit on pirates.

Meacham, Jon. *Thomas Jefferson: President and Philosopher*. New York: Crown Books for Young Readers, 2014.

Meltzer, Milton. *Piracy and Plunder: A Murderous Business*. New York: Dutton Children's Books, 2001.

Platt, Richard. *Pirate,* Eyewitness. New York: DK Publishing, 2004.

Selected Sources

This book could not exist without primary sources. The most essential were the letters, the journals, and the ships' logs left by the participants. These are collected in *Naval Documents Related to the United States Wars with the Barbary Powers* (Washington: U.S. Govt. Print. Off, 1939–44). The documents take up six volumes.

Adult books of particular use in creating this Young Readers Edition include:

Abbot, Willis. *The Naval History of the United States.* New York: Dodd, Mead and Company, 1896.

Kitzen, Michael. *Tripoli and the United States at War: A History of American Relations with the Barbary States, 1785–1805.* Jefferson, NC: McFarland & Co., Inc., 1992.

Lambert, Frank. *The Barbary Wars: American Independence in the Atlantic World.* New York: Hill and Wang, 2005.

London, Joshua. *Victory in Tripoli: How America's War with the Barbary Pirates Established the U.S. Navy and Shaped a Nation.* New York: John Wiley & Sons, Inc., 2005.

Magoun, F. Alexander. *The Frigate Constitution and Other Historic Ships.* New York: Dover Publications, 1987.

Martin, Tyrone G. *A Most Fortunate Ship: A Narrative History of Old Ironsides.* Annapolis, MD.: Naval Institute Press, 2003.

Books on the Subject Intended for the Middle School Reader:

Forester, C. S. *The Barbary Pirates*. New York: Sterling Publishing Company, 2007.

Hakim, Joy, and Diane L. Brooks. *Making Thirteen Colonies*, 3rd ed.New York: Oxford University Press, 2005.

Lawson, Don. *Morocco, Algeria, Tunisia, and Libya*. New York: Franklin Watts, 1978.

Lock, Deborah. *Pirate*. New York: DK Publishing, 2005.

Stein, R. Conrad, and Tom Dunnington. *The Story of the Barbary Pirates*. Chicago: Children's Press, 1982.

Wachtel, Roger. *Old Ironsides*. New York: Children's Press, 2003.

In addition, the websites of the U.S. Navy (https://www.navy.mil) and the U.S. Marine Corps (https://www.marines.mil) provide thorough history and images.

Photo Credits

Index